DREAM MAKERS

Surround Yourself with the Best to Be Your Best

JIM "THE ROOKIE" MORRIS
AND MARK STUERTZ

SAVIO
REPVBLIC

A SAVIO REPUBLIC BOOK
An Imprint of Post Hill Press
ISBN: 978-1-68261-796-0
ISBN (eBook): 978-1-68261-797-7

Dream Makers:
Surround Yourself with the Best to Be Your Best
© 2020 by Jim "The Rookie" Morris and Mark Stuertz
All Rights Reserved

Cover Design by Jomel Cequina

posthillpress.com
New York • Nashville
Published in the United States of America

To my beautiful wife,

Shawna

For being right beside me through the good
times, great times, and struggles.
You have shown me what true love is, and
our journey continues.

TABLE OF CONTENTS

Jimmy Morris has a way of taking lemons and making lemonade. Those lemons can be coming at him like fastballs in rapid succession. It doesn't matter. He faces whatever life throws at him with grace and humility. He never gives up. And his way of being has had a profound impact on me, both as an actor and as a human being. His trajectory in many ways paralleled my own journey.

I had a lightening start to my acting career. I was blessed to be a part of projects that were both commercially and critically successful including *Breaking Away* (1979), *The Right Stuff* (1983), and *The Big Easy* (1986). But after *Great Balls of Fire* (1989), the pressures of success and fame took a toll on me. I entered rehab in an effort to conquer a cocaine addiction. Through it all, I was confident that I was doing the right thing, that my life was going to improve. But sometimes you've got to be careful what you ask God for because he often presents you with challenging tests instead of what you might see as opportunities.

I took a year off to get a good hold of my life. That year wound up being two. Getting sober was a very humbling experience and I took my time trying to find the right film script, one that would get my career back on track.

But it wasn't to be. I ended up making some poor film choices along the way and my career fell into a slump that lasted several years.

It didn't begin to rebound until I took part in the Disney production of *The Parent Trap* (1998), which was followed by *The Rookie* (2002). Like *The Parent Trap*, *The Rookie* was both a critical and box office success. But it was much more than that. It was a movie about second chances.

The Rookie gave me the inspiration for my second act. It paralleled my own life and spiritual journey, a story about achieving impossible dreams after enduring dark periods of being tested in the wilderness. *The Rookie* is about achieving something you never even thought of as a possibility. That's what God does. You may think you're going after this or that, but what you eventually end up with is much different, something unexpectedly deeper and more profound.

By the time *The Rookie* fell into my lap, I had not played baseball since I was a kid in Little League, where I was a pitcher and a first baseman. I hadn't thrown a ball in years. But I had five months to prepare for the role. I worked with Los Angeles Dodgers catcher Paul Lo Duca who would come over to my house and train with me in my front yard. After a month of doing that, I got the opportunity to go to Dodgers Stadium every Friday afternoon and pitch on the mound in an empty ballpark.

Talk about an unexpected dream coming true: I never even imagined being on the same mound as greats like Sandy Koufax, Don Drysdale, and Fernando Valenzuela. By the time we started shooting the film, my pitching had become respectable, though I never put myself on a radar gun.

I think people, especially artists and athletes, need to remake themselves every seven years. Like crabs, lobsters, or snakes, we need to shed our old skins in order to grow. Otherwise you get stuck.

We also need to remake ourselves spiritually. Too often, we settle into the same things until it all just becomes rote words and ritual. There's no meaning in it. And that's really what *The Rookie* did for me. It refreshed me spiritually. It forced me to reexamine who I was and what I was doing. It filled my life with meaning. I began to feel like myself again.

Jimmy was an inspiration throughout the filming process. Just being around him was all I needed to slip into character. He's an extremely humble person and he naturally expresses the kind of humility that comes from braving life's most difficult trials. Yet despite the lows he has endured, Jimmy maintains a positive outlook animated by a wickedly infectious sense of humor. He radiates that to other people.

Working with Jimmy was a life-changing journey for me, and after that experience I gave up trying so hard. I let go of a lot of emotional baggage and issues I had with my own father, my career, and other circumstances in my life that I hadn't yet dealt with. I was able to be myself and get out of my own way.

The amazing thing is that, after *The Rookie*, opportunities started showing up, seemingly without much effort on my part. Life got easier. It's something that I can't explain.

Jimmy Morris is a truly great human being, a man of great depth and faith. He changed my life. For the better. And if you let him in, I'm confident he will do the same for you.

- Dennis Quaid

INTRODUCTION

As a speaker I have been given many opportunities to share my story, a tale that's beautiful at times, ugly at others. Yet all of the experiences I retell have made me who I am, who I believe my grandparents—the most formative influences in my life—wanted me to be.

When I reflect on how I have gotten to this point, I realize I've made many choices, some good, others disastrous. And from the time I stepped out on the mound at the Ballpark in Arlington, Texas at the age of thirty-five, I have come to one conclusion: I would not change a thing, because life is about the journey, not the destination.

As a person of faith, I know my final destination. It's everything in between that has made me who I am, and what I will continue to grow into. Baseball is a big part of this. I love the feel of the ball slipping out of my fingers, the smell of the leather glove on my hand, and the slapping pop of a fastball striking the catcher's mitt.

I love the green manicured grass and the smell of hotdogs, popcorn, and beer. Baseball was my dream. Your senses are at their sharpest on the baseball diamond, taking in all of the saturated colors, the crystal-clear sounds (the bat cracks, the cheers, the organ), and the heady scents. It all boils down to the indescribable charm of being a grown up playing a kid's game.

Yet baseball is just an entrée to my story. For those not interested in the game, this book (and my speeches) offers so much more. It's about dreams. It's about how to set yourself up for success. It's about how to empathize with and be of service to those around you—that person next to you, for instance.

It's about love, happiness, fortitude, grace, humility, respect, and being the best you that you can be in any given moment. It's about the rollercoaster of life.

It's about being overwhelmed by chronic illness. It's hard to describe what it's like being an elite athlete. The body is a symphony of super sharp senses, finely tuned reflexes, and precisely controlled movements. To this, add the ability to push the body to its absolute limits without (seemingly) breaking a sweat. Being in that zone—there's no feeling like it in the world. It's the ultimate high.

To suddenly lose this level of physical ability is pure devastation. Before I was diagnosed with Chronic Traumatic Encephalopathy (CTE)-induced Parkinson's disease, my senses and reflexes were in rapid decline, a much faster descent than the simple aging process would dictate.

My sense of taste and smell disappeared. I had trouble balancing. Turning my body around in a 360-degree circle became impossible. I couldn't pass squarely through a doorway without banging into the doorjamb on one side or the other. My leg dragged when I walked, and I was tripping constantly. I was like a shiny human ball in a pinball machine—bong, bong.

My kids started to take notice after I fell off a ladder in the attic and crashed into a box of Christmas decorations while attempting to change a furnace filter. Once, after watching a video of a speech I had given, my daughters asked me a question.

"Dad, why don't you make facial expressions anymore when you speak?"

I hadn't noticed. I had lost the ability to work the muscles beneath the skin of my face. It's called the "Parkinson's Mask," a blank look on the face. You stare.

What was causing this? Was my body getting back at me for the years of abuse I had dished it through competitive exertion and ignored healing times? Or was God trying to get my attention?

The thing I realized after suffering through these ordeals was that God could take a mess like me and work incredible wonders. No matter how much life had kicked me around, no matter how many wrong decisions I made or how many injuries and surgeries I had endured, there was redemption. There was healing. When it was all about me things never worked out. When it became about everything but me—my own kids, the students in my classroom, the players on my high school baseball team—my dream came true.

Only then, I believe, did God know I was ready. He got my attention. He gave me my lifelong dream of playing baseball in the Major Leagues. Now I share my life story with people around the world.

I recently gave a speech in California before a group of employees from a software firm. After my talk, a man pulled me aside as we were leaving the room. He whispered to me so that nobody else could hear.

"I want you to know that I was the guy in the back of the room crying," he admitted. "When you were talking about your grandfather, it brought back memories of my own grandfather."

He told me that when he was fifteen, his parents moved the family from Saudi Arabia to Pakistan to care for his ailing grandfather. They tended to him for more than two years until the day he died, and through this process he grew to love him deeply.

"He was the best person I have ever known," he said. "There were more than twenty thousand people at his funeral. I'm Muslim, but I understand where you are coming from. You need to keep doing what you are doing."

I gave another speech not many years before, and after all of the business people I had spoken to took pictures with me and left, a young woman approached me. She was in tears.

"I want you to know that after my husband left me, I took my kids to see your movie," she said. "Because of what your story meant to me, I decided to go to medical school. I am now graduating and I'm buying my kids their first house."

She told me how she struggled to put herself through school with three small children, waiting tables to feed them. My story gave her the faith to persist and reach her dream. It's hard to describe the impact these stories have on me, how deeply they touch me. It's how I know I'm on the right path.

After having spoken to so many different groups over the last twenty years, I know this: everyone has a story that makes their own journey unique; everyone has a dream that is within their grasp.

I have failed at many things in my lifetime. I have failed more than I have succeeded. But I do know this: if we are failing, we are living; we are trying. And those attempts will eventually lead to success.

Remember, the dream you start chasing may not be the dream you end up loving the most.

CHAPTER 1

MOUND OF DREAMS

It was late afternoon, sunny and searing. The mercury had clawed its way up to 103 degrees. The baseball stadium was packed. I felt an incredible rush that day, being in my home state and in my favorite ballpark. But I didn't think there was any way the Tampa Bay Devil Rays were going to put me in. I figured they'd just let me adjust to this new reality for a couple of days. I had never in my entire life thrown a pitch in a big league game. Besides, I was thirty-five years old. I had just thrown three days in a row in AAA. I had finally gotten the best of the White Sox hitters I faced after they had worn me out in the previous series. There was just no way.

Then, in the bottom of the eighth inning, I got the call to warm up. *Me?* I thought. *Yeah, they just want me to throw a few pitches in front of forty thousand people in my home state. That's cool.*

Even through the tryouts, and in AA with all the front office guys scrutinizing me every time I released a pitch, and then in AAA with everyone coming to watch me pitch, I kind of settled on the idea that maybe I wasn't too old. But still…

There were 150 people with ties to me at the Ballpark at Arlington on that September day in 1999. I later found out that the Rangers manager Johnny Oats had let those people in for free. I was back at home. I saw my three kids for the first time in three months. The high school kids I coached were there. People I went to college with were there. It suddenly became tangible. *This is real now*, I thought. This was happening. And people saw it. Everyone I knew and loved was there to watch me live out my childhood dream.

Then I got the call.

The Texas Rangers were in first place. I had talked to a lot of big league pitchers about the different hitters the Rangers had at the time, what they swung at and how, what flustered them, and how to get by them. It was the bottom of the eighth inning. Center fielder Tom Goodwin was the runner on first. Shortstop Royce Clayton was up. There were two outs. We were down six to two.

I remember running from the bullpen to the pitcher's mound, seeing every movement in the stands in stark detail. I could hear everything that was being said. All of the colors in the stands were unusually clear and vivid. But once I got to the mound and the manager, Larry Rothschild, dropped the ball in my mitt, all I could see was my catcher, John Flaherty. Everything closed down on me. It was the most bizarre thing.

Rothschild said something to me, but I don't remember what it was. It didn't register. Flaherty and I talked about signs, and then I took my warm-up pitches.

Stupid things go through your head when you're in high pressure, high profile performance situations. I was absolutely terrified. I thought, *man this is a long way away from*

Big Lake, Texas. When you're on the mound with a high school team and there are just a few people in the stands, that's one thing. When you're in the Major Leagues and 40,000 people are bearing their eyeball gaze down on you, that's something completely different.

So, I basically came to a decision. I took a few deep breaths and said to myself, "If he hits a home run, that proves I'm here. If I get him out, that proves I'm here. Same difference." I had to convince my brain that the distance wasn't any further than it was on a high school baseball field. The surroundings are just bigger. The environment is larger. Much larger. I took my warm-up pitches. I was fine.

Clayton stepped into the batter's box. I couldn't hear anything. It was dead silent. My friend Roberto Hernandez, the Devil Rays right-handed reliever, said "Man, they were talking about you on the big screen TV and everyone was laughing and clapping." I didn't hear any of that.

My first pitch was a fastball, low and away. Clayton swung through for strike one. That throw was clocked at 96 miles per hour. My second pitch was another fastball that grazed the outside of the plate. That registered at 98. He took it for strike two.

He fouled the third pitch over the first base dugout. The count was 0-2. I wound up and unleashed my fourth pitch, another 98-mile-per-hour fastball that streaked by Clayton's chest. He wound up and quickly checked his swing. Flaherty appealed to the first base umpire. He ruled the bat crossed the plate. Strike three. Clayton didn't argue the call.

I retired the side with four pitches. It all felt so smooth. Steve Canter, my agent, said it looked like my feet weren't even touching the ground when I was coming off the mound.

"It looked like you were exploding into the ball," he said. "Cool," I replied.

I was pushing into the ball so hard my feet actually lifted off the mound. I earned the nickname "easy gas" because it didn't even look like I was trying to throw the ball hard. Yet those pitches would hit speeds in the high 90s.

When I came off the mound it was like I was walking on air. In the dugout, Flaherty tossed me the strikeout ball. "You might want this," he said. Everyone was slapping me on the back and giving me high fives.

If this was something that had happened to me at nineteen, I would be like, "Hey, I'm good. I deserve this." But at thirty-five, having been out of the game for so long, coming back, and being able to experience that moment after having lived so much of life and having been humbled by its struggles, it's something you can't even put into words. You nurture a dream when you're a kid. When that moment actually happens, it's so much better than a dream could ever be.

∞

Before I released my first pitch in the Major Leagues, my first thought was how long it had taken me to get there and that it was worth every day that I'd spent trying to reach that point. Scaling that mound was like climbing a mountain, a peak that took more than a quarter century to summit.

Two days after that game against Texas, I pitched in Anaheim against the Angels. They brought me in in the seventh inning. Big hitters Jim Edmonds and Tim Salmon grounded out. Then I got Mo "the Hit Dog" Vaughn to hit a

95-mile-an-hour rocket to our centerfielder. Three up, three down. The next time I faced Vaughn, I made him look silly. I struck him out and the momentum from his swing made him lose his balance and fall down.

The first few innings I pitched, I didn't give up a single hit. I think people were shocked at this because of my age. Why is this guy throwing so hard?

Two years later, Tom Goodwin—the runner on first in my inaugural game against Texas—and I were together at spring training with the Dodgers. We were in the training room together before practice one day, and he walked up to me and put his arm around me. "You are not allowed to pitch to me," he said.

The most gratifying moments in baseball came when everything just clicked, throwing the ball the way that I did. If I was facing a right-handed batter and I threw the ball at his left side, it would tail back and cut across the plate. They would just look at me and go, "Whoa, what the hell was that?"

There were days I would go out and I knew without a doubt: nobody's touching my fastball. It's a feeling that you have, how the ball comes out of your hands, how it effortlessly slips through your fingertips. You're hurting the catcher's hand, but it doesn't even feel like you're throwing at all.

And then there are days when you have to gut it out, like you couldn't break a pane of glass with your hardest throw. But you have to go out and do it anyway. It's about knowing your body, and what you're able to do day in and day out. I learned very quickly from the other pitchers that relievers have to have a short memory. If you do well one day, you have to flush it and get ready for the next game. If you do poorly, you have to forget it and be ready for the next day. You can't get too high or too low. It's a mental toughness you learn over time.

In my senior year of high school during the district championship, we were down to the finals and all we had to do was win one out of two games to capture the title. The first night, I couldn't throw over the plate to save my life. The ball was going all over the place. I walked fifteen people. We lost by a score of ten to nine.

The very next night and with a sore arm I pitched again, and struck out twenty-one players. We shut them out five to nothing. What's the difference? I had to own up to what I could and couldn't do that second night, because I didn't have the arm I had the night before. I had to stay in control of my body and remain focused on what I had, knowing there was no way I was going to throw a fastball past anybody. So—it's a thinking man's game.

It's all about your mindset and the realization that you've really got to work your game when you don't have all of the usual weapons in your arsenal. The trick is learning to recognize and finesse your capabilities on any given day.

I grew up watching baseball. I played in tournaments and on traveling teams. I learned what an intricate game it is—literally a game of inches. If a ball is two inches one way, it's a double. If it's two inches the other way, it's a foul ball and doesn't count.

Stepping into the batter's box is the toughest thing on the planet for an athlete. Pitchers get do overs. If you didn't get the desired revolutions on the ball this time, just throw it again. Hitters have to calibrate all of that—speed, spin, timing—in their brain while they're in the box watching the pitcher release the ball. Do I swing or do I let it go by? Batters who can adjust to something coming at them faster than the blink of an eye, who can instantly make the decision to swing through and solidly make contact with the ball, those are the most talented athletes in the world.

Even elite golfers—who are fantastic—hit a stationary object, and they screw up a lot. Good hitters, those that have the reaction time and the ability to know what they're going to do, make up their mind and actually execute all in miniscule fractions of a second, that's a feat that's incomprehensible to me.

I love the game of baseball. That's why I taught it. I used it as a teaching tool everywhere I went. I believe life coincides with baseball. There are disappointments, there are joys, and there are come-from-behind victories. There are ways you can set up your life in which you load the bases, and then all of the sudden you make three outs and strand your opportunities, leaving you right back where you started. There are also those times when you just get up and swing for the fences and everything seems to be a homerun.

When I first got into the Major League farm system as a kid, I couldn't throw hard. I was herky-jerky. I didn't have control. My pitches were maybe 87 or 88 miles per hour. Once in a great while I would hit 90.

At the age of twenty-eight while playing football for Angelo State University, I had shoulder surgery where my surgeon, Dr. Vernon Ryan, removed a three-inch bone spur from my rotator cuff and repaired the joint. The bone spur had destroyed my deltoid muscle, and Dr. Ryan cut 85 percent of that muscle out of my left shoulder. He told me that I would never pitch again. But God!

When I came back, I not only threw hard, all of the sudden I had control. Back in Big Lake, Texas, I was pitching every day to my high school team. I worked on being smooth because it was easier for me to observe and judge their swings from the pitcher's mound than it was from behind the plate. The smoothness I developed was for the benefit of those kids, and to take pressure off my arm so that I could easily throw again for them the next day. I did not have that ability to begin with.

Major League Baseball is essentially a brotherhood of those who are really good at something, good enough to compete with the best athletes in the world. That's just a feeling you can't get anywhere else. Good lawyers may tell you they get that feeling in the courtroom after they've won a case. Well, I'm not a lawyer, so I don't get that. But I sure do get it with baseball.

The baseball diamond was the one place that I knew without a doubt I was successful. No matter what my abusive father said to me when I was growing up, no matter how many times he told me I was stupid, or that I sucked, or that I would never amount to anything, in between those white lines he didn't exist. I could go and play the game I loved, and it would be more than worth it. Every second of it. When you end up on that field playing with and competing against the absolute best in the world, that must mean that you're pretty good too.

CHAPTER 2

MOUND OF NIGHTMARES

I played football with the legendary Gordon Wood, the coach of the Brownwood Lions football team. Wood coached for forty-three seasons, winning or sharing twenty-five district championships and nine state championships. His overall record as coach was an astounding 396 wins to 91 losses and 15 ties. He was inducted into the Texas High School Coaches Hall of Fame and the Texas Sports Hall of Fame in 1983. In 1999, the *Dallas Morning News* named Gordon Wood "Coach of the Century."

But if truth be told, I hated the guy. I broke my ankle once on the basketball court and he berated me with an offensive slur and made me get up. He said I was embarrassing him. He didn't know my ankle was broken, and probably didn't care. The pain brought tears to my eyes. The following day I was in a cast.

Coach Wood often told me I would never make it in baseball because I was destined to be a football player. He hated baseball, especially when compared to his first love: the gridiron. Plus, I think he carried a grudge against me from the days when my father played for him. Though he was an exceptionally talented athlete, he bailed out of the team after just two weeks. My father was a quitter. Coach Wood would tell us all the time that there are winners and losers and "never-will-be's."

"Your father was a never-will-be," he would say to me.

I did excel at the game. If I had stuck it out, doing the things I did on the high school football field, I would have gone on to a Division I college team as a quarterback. Coach Wood wanted me to go to Arkansas. As I was taller than Drew Brees (at 5'11"), I would have been drafted into the NFL. I have no doubt about this. I ran the 40-yard dash in 4.4 seconds, I could throw the ball 85 yards, and I could catch anything. Plus: I was an especially skilled punter and kickoff specialist—the resident aliens of the football team. I could have done whatever I wanted to on the football field.

In the football quarterfinals my senior year, I separated my shoulder diving for a ball on artificial turf, back when artificial turf was nothing but concrete with stiff fuzz on top. I landed with my arm extended trying to catch a pass, and my weight, combined with the mass of the defensive back on top me, pushed my shoulder hard into the turf, dislocating the joint.

As I lay on the ground in agony, Coach Wood walked out onto the field. "Are you hurt, or are you injured?" he asked. When you've got a coach who calls you every curse word in the book when you think you're too hurt to play, well, you simply have to prove him wrong. So, they popped my shoulder back into place and I went back into the game.

At practice the next morning, I wanted to scream every time I got hit or I landed on my shoulder. Two days later, I sang the "Hallelujah Chorus" with the school choir at the coliseum in Brownwood. My arm was in a sling and I was doped up on pain pills. I was propped up in the back row of the choir with my best friend holding onto my left elbow and my other friend, a tight end on the football team, holding me up on the right. I was sweating like all get out because I was in so much pain and unable to stand. But there I was, dressed in a tux singing the "Hallelujah Chorus" because that was what we were expected to do. And that is what we did.

Coach Wood got my doctor to write a note clearing me to play. So I did, albeit with a cortisone injection. I was expected to play and when you're a team player, you take one for your team. I played the next two-and-a-half games with my upper arm strapped to my side with athletic tape. When you're a receiver and a punter, that rig doesn't work out too well. I would go on to have four surgeries on that shoulder years later. One of my receptions was a one-handed catch. I jumped up high into the air, spinning as I clutched the ball and pulled it into my body. My teammate, Mike Kinsey—a defensive back and the toughest guy I ever knew—ran over to pick me up off the field. "I have never seen anything like that before in my life," he said.

Okay, maybe hate is a strong word. I did not hate Coach Wood as much as I disagreed with him. I liked football, but I loved baseball. I respected Coach Wood because his expectations were high. All of these years later, I realize he is one of the best motivators and high school football coaches to have ever lived. He made us men.

It's funny when you look back at your life and ask yourself—what if? By the age of twenty-four I was out of baseball, believing that maybe Coach Wood was right—*I'd never make it in baseball.*

At twenty-seven and twenty-eight I played college football at Angelo State University, and made Kodak All-American in Division II as a punter. I had soft hands and a 5.3-second hang time. Several NFL teams came through town and talked to me. I had high hopes. But the draft in 1993 came and went and I wasn't selected. I was crushed.

Jump ahead ten years. With a book and a movie on my resume, I was building a successful career as a motivational speaker. I was in Corpus Christi one evening speaking before the Hispanic Chamber of Commerce. Reed Ryan, son of baseball great Nolan Ryan, was there to announce that the Hooks, a minor league baseball team affiliated with the Houston Astros, was coming to town.

Following my speech that night, a man approached me. He introduced himself and asked if I remembered him.

"No sir," I replied. "I've met a lot of people over the last few years."

He told me he was my football agent when I punted in college. He explained that when he heard I was coming to Corpus, he pulled out some of my old game films and reviewed them.

"I came here to ask you a question," he said. "When the Steelers were going to draft you in the second round to punt and kickoff, why didn't you return the call?"

I stood there with my jaw on the ground, stunned. "What?" I asked.

He went on to explain that the Pittsburg Steelers wanted me and had left a message for me to call them back, but that I never returned their call. I never got that message. Hence, I went undrafted. I guess God had other plans.

My descent from the mound began almost as abruptly as my ascent. I remember the last game of the 1999 season in St. Petersburg, where the Devil Rays faced the Yankees. We were playing to close our season. The Yankees were playing for a lot more that year. They were destined for the playoffs and the team went on to win the World Series in four games against the Atlanta Braves. They called me to the mound in the fifth inning. I gave up one hit and had one strikeout after facing four batters in a game that we went on to win by a score of 6 to 2.

By the time I took a shower and got to the airport to go home, I had come down with laryngitis, bronchitis, and an upper respiratory infection, all in a matter of two hours. I was worn out. I had been working out like I hadn't since I was a teen. That, combined with telling my story more times than I could remember, pushed me over the edge. After three months of constant everything, this old ball-player was rendered numb from exhaustion.

At the conclusion of that first season, I came back and broke camp with the Devil Rays in 2000. In January, before spring training began, several ball players, including my best friend Roberto (Bert) Hernandez, and me toured South Florida by bus to get the fans pumped up for baseball season.

"Are you ready to cry?" Bert asked me. I had no idea what he meant, but I would soon find out. Our stops included hospitals. Those hospitals had oncology wings—no surprise. What I was not ready for was the children's oncology wing.

For us big bad professional ballplayers, that was over-whelming. These brave kids were amazing. They smiled.

We took pictures, gave them hugs, and signed autographs for them. We were reduced to tears—Hall of Fame third baseman Wade Boggs, all-star first baseman Fred McGriff, Bert, a few others, and me. We got to run around playing a game while these kids were fighting for their lives. My only question was: who were the kids and who were the adults?

A few weeks later, spring training began and that's when I got my first inkling that something in my body was amiss. It started benignly: stiff neck, sinus infection, and a headache. When I look back now, I wasn't recovering as quickly from ailments as I normally did. So, I washed down some Advil with wine—my own prescription—and got back at it.

I broke camp with the big league team, and all seemed normal. As the only lefty in the bullpen, I pitched a lot but was not always put in the game. I would warm up, then sit down. Warm up, sit down. Sometimes I got in the game. Sometimes I didn't.

On May 9, 2000, in a game against the Yankees at Yankee stadium, my elbow started hurting. I came into the game in the bottom of the tenth inning with the bases loaded. The score was tied 3 to 3. It was the fourth time I had been on the mound in four days. Yankee right fielder Paul O'Neil, who I later learned was deathly afraid of me, came into the batter's box. I walked O'Neil in four pitches, unleashing meatballs at 86 to 87 miles per hour. I walked in the winning run.

I simply couldn't throw the ball. Pitchers talk about having a dead arm. My arm was pushing up daisies. It didn't matter if I tried to throw hard or not; I clocked in at 87 miles per hour and simply couldn't push beyond that barrier.

I always had the ability to recuperate quickly after wearing out my arm and I generally wasn't sore the next day. But after that Yankees game, my arm didn't bounce back like it had in the past. I never pitched again in the Major Leagues.

"He is the only lefty we've got," Bert told the manager. "You guys are killing him. Stop it. He doesn't need to throw three or four times in a row."

So they sent me down to AAA in late May to rest and work on my pitching. After the move, I learned the Devil Rays traded for another lefty, Mark Guthrie, who played with the 1991 World Champion Minnesota Twins.

Rest helped. I faced the Phillies AAA team and was throwing 95 and 96 mph—the same rate I had thrown before.

Usually, when I threw hard, I could feel the ball come out of my fingertips. When I felt it come out like that, I knew I was in the zone just by how it felt on release. But when I threw against the Phillies, I didn't have that feeling, even though I had the speed. That's when I knew something was wrong. I looked down at my elbow and went "Uh, oh."

It had swelled up to the size of an apple. Turns out I had stretched the ligament in my elbow. A month later in June, I had surgery in Los Angeles to tighten and "loop" the ligament. The Devil Rays management got mad at me because I went to my own doctor, Frank Jobe, in Los Angeles instead using the Devil Rays team doctor. Jobe was an innovator. He'd performed the first "Tommy John" surgery in 1974 on the great Dodgers left-handed pitcher Tommy John after he needed the ulnar collateral ligament in his elbow repaired.

He pioneered the surgical procedure by grafting a tendon from another part of the body into the medial elbow.

Jobe also happened to be the Dodgers team doctor. So, after the Devil Rays cut me loose at the end of the season, Jobe advised the Dodgers to sign me. He told them I was in great shape. I was in rehab for the rest of 2000, going back and forth from my kids in Texas—eight year-old Hunter, four and a half year-old Jessica, and infant Jaimee—to Los Angeles where my doctor practiced.

The Dodgers signed me that winter to compete for a closer's role in the bullpen. It was a turbulent season filled with drama. Disney was laying the groundwork for the movie *The Rookie*, about my unlikely journey to the Major Leagues. My marriage to Lorri was over. I was separated from my kids.

It wasn't long after that, during spring training of 2001, that I started to notice I was having trouble judging balls thrown back at me after a pitch. During pepper exercises, where a batter hits brisk ground balls and line drives to a group of fielders standing nearby, I was having a hard time adjusting my eyes to the ball. Then I started having balance issues.

Since the Dodgers are a National League team, pitchers have to hit. When it was my turn in the batting cages, all I was asked to do was bunt. Catch the ball with the barrel of the bat. Make simple contact to advance a runner. But I couldn't even do that. In fact, I was so bad that instead of the ball hitting the bat, it hit my right thumb and broke it—equal parts embarrassing and aggravating. I said a lot of four-letter words.

It happened all at once, like the flick of a light switch. In the span of just two weeks, I lost everything. Among my greatest fears in baseball was being on the pitcher's mound facing some great big all-star and, after throwing a meatball, he hits a line drive at my noggin and I can't get out of the way. I'm throwing pitches at close to 100 miles per hour, but I can't even judge a bunt. I was afraid someone was going to smoke me in the teeth.

On top of that, I was going through a divorce (from a marriage that was doomed from the start due to incompatibility, but we had to prove everyone wrong who saw what we didn't), I was in a custody battle for my kids, I was about to take part in the production of *The Rookie*, and then there was this baseball thing. I did it. I made it to the Big Leagues. But, I concluded, it was time to move on.

So I walked into manager Jim Tracy's office, and I said, "Look, I appreciate everything you have done for me. You guys are a great organization. But my kids are more important. I'm never going to light the world on fire in baseball. I got to play the game I love for that brief period and I appreciate the opportunity. But it's more important for to me to go home and watch my kids grow up and live their dreams."

And this big league manager, with all of the pressures he was facing with the mercurial personalities on his roster, got up and walked around his desk and gave me a hug.

"Man, if only I had more like you," he said. "If you ever need anything, you call me." He then sent the club house kid through the locker room to collect hats, bats, balls, and batting gloves to give to my kids when I got home.

And that was that. I was done. I was relieved. There was a lot of pressure going from a high school classroom to being a member of a professional sports organization, giving interviews to every newspaper and TV station on the planet over the course of just a few months. I may not have had the opportunity to play with a hall of fame team over a twelve-year career, but I struck out some of the best players ever to play the game. I love baseball, and will always have a passion for it. But I never looked back. I went home, got my kids, and headed to the movie set. There, we got to hang out with movie stars, a top-flight movie production team, and meet some incredible people along the way. I regret none of it.

⁓

The next episode in my downward spiral occurred after Disney sent Dennis Quaid—the actor who played me in *The Rookie*—and me on a publicity tour. We were doing some interviews in Fort Worth and I pulled out my cell phone and couldn't see the numbers. I've had 20/15 vision over the course of my entire life. Now I couldn't even see the dial panel on my phone. What the hell's going on?

And then the headaches started. These were throbbing aches that wouldn't let up. My neck started locking up. Within five months of quitting baseball, I had issues with balance, eyesight, fatigue, and these recurrent, pounding headaches. When I was on an airplane and would reach down to pick up something after I had dropped it, my shoulder would separate and my arm would buckle. I'd sit back up and my shoulder would slip back into place. The pain raged through my arm like wildfire.

In one instance, as I was walking through Dallas-Fort Worth International Airport, talking to my new wife Shawna while holding the phone in my left hand and gripping a suitcase in my right, my whole right shoulder gave out. My upper arm had separated from my shoulder blade. I immediately turned white from the searing, stabbing pain. I'm not sure if I dropped my suitcase, but I'm pretty sure I blurted out the "F" word.

That's how it all began. I lived in a constant state of exhaustion, a persistent state of agonizing pain. I was driving my wife and my kids crazy because they didn't know what was wrong with me. I didn't know what was wrong with me.

I remember in 2002, just after Shawna and I got married in a small ceremony with family and friends, I was having lunch with our pastor, Scott Sager, from Preston Road Church of Christ in Dallas' University Park. I asked him, "Scott? Why couldn't I have started here at this place in my life? I love my wife and she loves me. I love my kids. They're happy. They love my wife. I feel like I've made so many mistakes in the past. Why couldn't we have just started here?"

He looked me dead in the eye and said, "Jimmy, you don't know how good *good* is until you see how bad *bad* can be." I had no idea how long bad would last, or how awful the experience would be.

CHAPTER 3

JOURNEY TO THE DREAM

When I was just a toddler, my dad got an assignment that sent him to sea for several months. So, my mom packed me up into the car and we made the trip from Key West, where my dad was stationed, to San Saba, Texas to visit her mother. San Saba is about 105 miles northwest of Austin.

My grandmother was thrilled to see her only grandson. She bought me a closet full of toys—cars, guns, and tanks. But I wasn't much interested in these things. What my mother had neglected to tell her was that I mostly played with balls. I loved balls of all kinds. I loved holding them, rolling them, throwing them, bouncing them, and catching them. Give me a toy truck and I'd quickly toss it aside, crying out for a ball.

My grandmother took note. After my dad returned from his assignment and just before my third birthday, she came for her first visit to Key West. And she came bearing gifts—a junior baseball uniform. The ensemble contained a cap, shirt, and pants, all with "Little Slugger" embroidered on them. There was also a tiny glove, a soft baseball with red laces painted on it, and a small bat. I begged my mother to play with me. I connected with her first pitch and the ball sailed over her head.

From then on, the ball, glove, and bat went everywhere I did. I begged people to pitch to me or let me pitch to them. I'd toss the ball up in the living room trying to see how close I could get to the ceiling without touching it, and practice catching it in my mitt on the way down. At night, I'd lie on my back in bed and toss the ball up and catch it over and over.

As I grew, my passion intensified. I always wanted to throw better, catch better, and hit better than anybody else. Baseball was something I could do all by myself. That's a big plus for someone who was an introvert and didn't talk much. I often played with a tennis ball. I could throw the ball hard off a wall and practice catching line drives of grounders on the bounce back. I played Fungo—tossing the ball in the air and swinging at it with a bat—to practice hitting. I tossed balls on the roof of buildings and let them roll off—sometimes popping up when they struck the gutter—to practice catching pop flies.

Because my father was in the navy, we moved around all of the time, relocating to bases across the country, settling mostly in military housing. We went from Key West to San Pedro, California, to San Francisco, and back to San Pedro before returning to San Francisco where we quartered in the Presidio army base. After that we were sent to Naval Station Great Lakes near Waukegan, a town on Lake Michigan about an hour north of Chicago. We were there just long enough to take in the bone-chilling snow.

This constant locomotion was jarring to my young state of mind. Because I didn't talk much and we didn't stay in one spot long enough for me to forge friendships, my best friend was sports. The friends I did make came about after I showed up at a park or a yard with a ball and glove. The other kids were always impressed with my throwing and batting prowess.

We returned to Key West after our stay in Waukegan, three years after we left. As a seven-year-old, I played baseball all of the time. I'd play games in the city league with other kids from the navy base, and then come home and play games in somebody's yard.

A navy officer who had permanent shore duty converted his huge side yard into a little baseball field. When he came home from work, he'd umpire baseball games for the kids from the base. When I got frustrated at my inability to hit the ball, he gave me batting lessons.

My father loved baseball too, but he didn't have time to teach me the fundamentals of the game. So that officer took on the role of teaching me how to time pitches, swing the bat, and connect with the ball. I wanted to be at his house all the time because he treated me like a human being. When I was around my father, I was the dog who always got kicked. Baseball was my refuge, one of the true joys I had in my life. I doubt I would have successfully survived my childhood without it.

In Little League, I pitched and played first base. We lost every single game the first season I played. I got so frustrated; I quit before the last game. I couldn't tolerate being on a losing team.

My quick surrender came back to haunt me. Two weeks after the season ended, my mother forced me to go to the awards ceremony where the kid who replaced me at first base was to receive the All-Star award. I was red with resentment—embarrassment too. That honor would have been mine. In that moment, one lesson came crashing down on me: if you want to achieve anything, never quit because you never know what's around the corner. That was the first and only time I ever quit in my life.

Two years later, I moved with my family from Key West to New London, Connecticut. I was heartbroken. Key West had just begun to feel like home. When we arrived in New London to take up quarters in a townhouse complex, the air chafed with sub-zero temperatures and there was two feet of snow on the ground. Baseball was a distant memory.

Yet I learned most of the kids there followed the game, regularly taking in Red Sox, Yankees, and Mets games on the radio and TV. I played in military little league on the White Sox team, where I eventually became an all-star, making up for what I'd lost in Key West. There was a powerful right-hander on the Yankees team named Chip Cunningham. Cunningham was tall for his age, and few of the players in the league could hit off of his pitches. I was a hard-throwing left-hander and, as the new kid, an interloper on his hard-won turf. We became sworn enemies.

That animus reached its peak in one league game where we found ourselves locked in a pitcher's battle. He gave up just one hit. That hit came off of my bat, which enraged the right-hander. I battened his team down to zero hits, but it didn't matter. In the seventh inning when I walked a player, that on-base runner attempted to steal second. Our catcher overthrew the second basemen and the ball bounced into the outfield. The runner scored. We went down 1 to 0.

After that clash, all of the military team players struck up a game in that officer's yard with a bat and tennis ball. Cunningham and I continued our pitching duel on opposite teams. But from then on, we found ourselves on the same team in these games. No one could beat us. We became fast friends.

The baseball never stopped in that Connecticut neighborhood. We even played in the wintertime, catching and losing balls in the snow. We painted trashcan covers in bright colors to use as bases. In one of those games, we played with a foot of snow on the ground. Bundled up in winter jackets, we slipped and slid swinging at pitches, and rounded the bases sliding in thick slush, our breath unleashing puffs of fog. We used a batting helmet I had as home plate so that we could see it above the snow. That helmet was autographed by famed Red Sox slugger Fred Lynn. By the end of that game, my prized helmet was crushed.

But that was just the beginning of my memorabilia losses. After we ruined or lost all of our baseballs in the snow and slush, I was determined our game continue on. So I ran into the house and fetched one my baseballs, a ball that had been signed by Hall of Famer Henry Aaron. My prized baseball got destroyed.

I got both the batting helmet and the baseball at Fenway Park when our league all-star team took a field trip to watch the Milwaukee Brewers take on the Red Sox. Carlton Fisk hit two home runs that game, and Hank Aaron signed baseballs for us while Fred Lynn signed helmets.

When I turned eleven, we decamped from New London and moved to Virginia Beach where we lived for the greater part of a year. I hated the place. I had no friends. The local kids persecuted us military brats. At school I was verbally abused, tripped, and had my books pushed out of my hands. Adding to my turmoil was that I couldn't play base-ball because I had been diagnosed with Osgood-Schlatter disease, characterized by a painful bump just below the knee. Boys get this when they're too active for their immature bones. To treat the disease, doctors encased my right leg in a cast. That cast was on my leg for seven months.

Though my cast came off in time for the baseball season and I made the all-star team there, I couldn't wait to leave Virginia Beach behind. We left that God-forsaken place for Hollywood, Florida, where I attended Apollo Middle School, just a few blocks down from our house. At Apollo, I played baseball, basketball, and football, and ran track. I also played on the summer league team called the Italian Stallions. In the winter, the Stallions became a softball team, which was good enough to compete in state and national championships.

When I enrolled at McArthur High School, I became the second freshman ever in the history of the school to make the varsity baseball team. While I was on the McArthur baseball team, scouts from the University of Miami were observing my play and making plans to recruit me with a collegiate scholarship. The university team was a solid springboard into the pros. My Holly-wood dream was to play baseball for Miami before linking up with a professional ball club.

But it wasn't to be. That summer my father took a transfer to Brownwood, Texas to work as a navy recruiter, and I moved in with my grandparents before attending Brownwood High School. Brownwood High didn't have a baseball team. Leaving Hollywood and cutting off the possibility of actualizing my baseball dream was one of the most heartbreaking moments of my life.

The city of Brownwood lived and breathed football. So, I joined the football team and played with National High School Hall of Fame football coach Gordon Wood. I also pitched in the Brownwood summer city baseball league, despite the protestations of my father and my football coach. My father never thought I was any good at the game to begin with, and Coach Wood hated baseball. "I would rather watch grass grow," he would say.

During one city league night game, I hit three homeruns and struck out seventeen opposing players. But in my final appearance at bat, I went down swinging.

"You're not going to get any place hitting like that," my father said after the game. "You can't hit worth shit." Three homeruns. Seventeen strikeouts. What part of that isn't good?

My father and Coach Wood told me I would never make it in baseball. That discouragement just made me want to play the game all the more. I spent my whole life proving people—coaches, doctors, trainers, competing players, parents, and teachers—wrong. Sometimes, to my own lasting detriment.

⁓

I've always loved baseball. The game is like a chess match that mirrors life. If you can win in-between those white lines, you can win outside those lines too. I love the strategy, and the head games. I especially love the cat-and-mouse game of lineup changes for pinch hitters and relief pitchers, all designed to exploit the ideal pitcher-batter match-up. Most batters, after all, prefer to face an opposite handed pitcher.

Managers would put a left-handed batter in the on-deck circle so that when the opposing manager spots him, they'll burn a left-handed relief pitcher in the bullpen. But the player on deck won't really be the batter. At the last second, they'll put in a right-handed batter. So that the opposing team has warmed up the wrong guy.

In the meantime, you've got spotters around the field with binoculars trying to pick up catcher signs and coaching signals so that, for example, a batter will know ahead of time if a fastball or a breaking ball is coming. If there's a runner on second base, he might signal the batter. There are signs and signals bouncing all over the field.

The game of baseball has gone from Babe Ruth eating hot dogs, drinking beer, and promising to hit whatever the pitcher throws, to players and coaches analyzing every detail of the game. They scour game film, measure ball rotation speeds, and utilize data analytics to gain the slightest advantage. You almost have to be a physics teacher to manage and coach baseball these days. Sometimes I think we've lost the heart of America's National Pastime. Like everything else, it's all boiling down to digital—to ones and zeros.

The summer before my grandfather died, I received a letter from George Steinbrenner, legendary team owner of the New York Yankees. Apparently, a scout from the team had watched one of my summer league games and filed a report. They'd offered me a bare minimum deal—a few hundred dollars a month—in exchange for the long-shot slog to the top. I would have jumped at the chance if it weren't for my grandfather's declining health. I couldn't leave him.

I hadn't yet turned down the Yankees offer when Ranger Junior College baseball coach Jack Allen approached me after my last summer league game. An inductee into the American Baseball Coaches Association Hall of Fame, Allen was a legend. He'd turned down several offers to coach a pro team. He offered me a scholarship to play baseball at Ranger Junior College in Ranger, Texas. I accepted and played with the team until my grandfather passed away from Amyotrophic Lateral Sclerosis (ALS), or Lou Gehrig's disease, on the last weekend of November 1982.

After my grandfather's death, I knew it was time for me to get out of the house, mostly because my dad lived there. In January of 1983, the Milwaukee Brewers drafted me. They offered me $35,000 to play baseball. Having just turned nineteen, I knew far more than I did at eighteen.

I am rich, I thought to myself.

And for nine months, I was.

Now, a lot of dads would pour their hearts out to their sons when they leave home and head to Spring Training. They would say things that were encouraging, memorable, and impactful. They would understand that those words would be replayed over and over again in their son's head as he spends months away from home playing a game that constantly confronts you with failure. Wise dads would say things like:

"You can do this."

"Never give up. You'll make it."

"I'll be praying for you."

"I wish you all the best."

"I love you."

Instead, all my dad could muster was, "Do not go and buy a little red sports car."

After I bought my red five-speed Toyota Celica GT, I made the journey from Brownwood, Texas to Phoenix, Arizona for spring training. As I was making my way to my first-ever Spring Training in my first-ever sports car, I passed through Big Lake, Texas. I took in its baked dryland plains, its scrub and stands of cedar and mesquite, its ramshackle downtown strip, and the flaring oil well gas burn-off on the horizon. I was unimpressed.

Who in their right mind would live here? I thought to myself.

Apparently, God remembered that arrogant statement. "You will,"

He answered fifteen years later. My grandfather passed his strong faith on to me, and I can rest assured the Lord has a marvelous sense of humor.

After driving almost 1,000 miles, I pulled into the parking lot of the Brewers Spring Training camp in Phoenix. I spotted about 110 players congregating there and thought that represented the sum total of those reporting.

"In four months, you're gonna see me on TV," I boasted to my friends back home.

I later learned that those 110 ballplayers were just the pitchers.

Six weeks later, I finished Spring Training. I promptly received an invitation to "Extended Spring Training." Extended Spring Training is where they send you when you're not good enough to play on any minor league team.

I didn't understand how that was possible. Back in Brownwood, I struck out every player I ever faced in the city league games. No one could connect with my pitches. How was it possible that I couldn't even get one player out now? Even worse, I struggled throwing strikes. Baseball was the one thing I thought I was good at, and suddenly the cold truth was slapping me hard in the face: I was horrible.

After the June draft, when all the collegiate athletes were selected and offered significant signing bonuses, I was sent with these new draft picks to Rookie Ball in Paintsville, Kentucky. In truth, I was envious of these guys and their bonus money. I watched them work out for ten days before we got our seventy-two-game schedule. Through it all, I held to one persistent thought: *I will be the number one starter.*

It was the only move that made any sense. I had been in Extended Spring Training for close to six months. I was drafted first. I was paid first. I've been working hard and putting my heart into everything I've done. These college boys had just gotten out of school a few days before. Who were they?

At nineteen, I was a lot like a lot of other teenagers: the world was all about me; I was only going to be happy if things went my way.

When I didn't start the first game of the season, I was a little upset.

When I didn't start the second game, I got mad.

When I didn't start the third game, I threw a fit. I marched straight up to my manager and told him exactly what I was thinking.

"Look. I've been here for six months," I said with seething intensity. "You drafted me first. You obviously wanted me more. These guys just got out of school ten days ago. I've done everything I was supposed to. Why have I not started?"

His reply reflected the wisdom that comes from having been in and around the game for several seasons.

"Look, Jimmy, you'll start against the Braves Rookie League team tonight. If you do well enough, we'll change the rotation around just for you."

I didn't get the sarcasm at the time. They would never have done that, especially for me. After all, I wasn't exactly setting the radar guns on fire. We had a first, second, and third round draft pick there, all pitchers that eventually went to the big leagues. But because I had been there training with the team for the past six months, I thought I was better than I was.

"Thank you. I'm going to show you how good I am." I turned and walked away.

That game against the Braves Rookie League team was our fourth of the season. And I showed everyone just how good I was.

Only fifty-three pitches into the first inning, I had given up five home runs, sent three batters to first base on a hit by pitch, and walked everybody else. The manager was forced to pull me from the game, and I found myself sitting in the clubhouse with no outs. Not a strikeout, a pop out, or a ground out. Nothing. I was awful.

For the first time since my grandfather passed away, I sat alone and I cried. "But there's no crying in baseball," you might think. Yes, there is.

That night, I called my mom.

"I made a horrible mistake," I said to her. "I don't know what I was thinking. I should have played football. I'm quitting. I'm coming home. I'm done. I've wanted to do this my whole life, but I'm not any good."

"What would your grandfather say?" my mother asked. I was not expecting that reply. "What would Ernest say to someone who gave their word, promised to do something, signed a contract, and then walked away like it never existed? You're sticking it out, good or bad. You're not coming home. You are not welcome here Jimmy."

I thought about that for a good long time, the memory of my grandfather and his brave struggle with Lou Gehrig's Disease still fresh in my mind. So I did what my grandfather would have wanted me to do after giving my word. I stuck it out. For five-and-a-half years, I stuck it out. Through six surgeries, I stuck it out. And through all of that stick-to-itiveness, I never seemed to go anywhere. I never got above the level of single-A minor league ball.

Then, at the age of twenty-four, with agonizing pain in my elbow, I found myself sitting in the Birmingham, Alabama office of Dr. James Andrews, one of the top orthopedic surgeons in the world. I joked that he achieved this distinction by practicing on me all of the time.

"Look, you're only twenty-four," he said, looking me dead in the eye. "If you want to play, I can fix it and get you back on the field. The decision is yours. What do you want to do?"

I thought for a good long time. I thought about where I had been for the last five years, where I hadn't gone, and what I might be missing.

"Doc, it's time to grow up," I said. "I need to go home and go to college. If I can't play the game I love, maybe I can teach it. I'm going to go to school and get a degree. Eventually I'll meet somebody, get married, start a family, get a house, and get a dog. That's my plan."

"That's a great plan," Dr. Andrews said. "Start with the dog."

So, I got a dog.

∞

In 1987 at the age of twenty-two, I married my first wife, Lorri. Probably a psychologist or psychiatrist could explain our attraction to each other much better than we could. We had very little in common. Everyone told us we were making a big mistake. So we got married. Just to prove everyone wrong.

In fairness to Lorri, I spent the early years of our marriage more focused on baseball than on us. In 1989, I tried going pro again with the Chicago White Sox. But once again, I failed to rise past the single-A minor leagues. Defeated, I decided it was time to focus on new opportunities.

Lorri took a position as an admissions recruiter at Angelo State University in San Angelo, Texas. I worked a series of odd jobs and took college courses at Howard Payne University in Brownwood. As a student, I helped the school bring their baseball program back to life. But all of that changed when the coaches from Angelo State recruited me as a punter and kicker for the school's football team.

While playing football, I majored in kinesiology and psychology. And for the first time in my life, I loved school. I found the coursework challenging but well within my intellectual capabilities. Better yet, I wanted to be there.

The rest of my life was the hard part. I worked three jobs in between classes, including positions as a dorm director at the school and as a security guard working the midnight to 8 a.m. shift. I also had coaching positions at Edison Junior High and San Angelo Central High. I slept three hours a night. I grew to love the away football games because I could take off a day of work, actually get some sleep while traveling, and then get up and play football.

Unlike baseball, football was good to me. I earned College Football All-America Team honors in 1992 for my kicking abilities. Still, my love of baseball kept me longing for the game.

At the end of my second football season with Angelo State, the relentless pain in my shoulder was becoming unbearable. At the age of twenty-eight, I had already had nine surgeries on my elbow and shoulder. Now the Angelo State team doctor was recommending I undergo my tenth. That's when I paid a visit to Dr. Vernon Ryan, a skilled orthoscopic surgeon.

"Jimmy, why did you quit playing?" Dr. Ryan asked. "You were only twenty-four years old and you just walked away from your dream. Why?"

"Doc, I've not thrown a baseball in three years because of the pain," I said. "If I roll over on my throwing shoulder in the middle of the night, I cannot go back to sleep. It hurts that bad."

"Okay, Jimmy. I'm going to make an incision less than an inch long, I'll see what's there, I'll fix it up, and you'll be good as new. If there is anything really wrong with you, I will wake you up and discuss it with you before going any further."

So, after he woke me up, we discussed it.

"You, my friend, have a problem," Dr. Ryan said.

My problem was that I had a three-and-a-half-inch bone spur in my shoulder. That spur had a fork in it, and one of the prongs was inside my rotator cuff and had destroyed the joint. He explained that he would have to shave the whole shoulder joint just to make it fit and work properly. The other prong was destroying my deltoid muscle, and the damage was so extensive that he would have to cut away 85 percent of the existing tissue.

"I could fix it, but you're not going to pitch good anymore," he said.

"I couldn't pitch good to begin with," I replied in a Demerol haze. "Don't worry about it."

When I awoke from surgery, that one-inch incision had grown to six-and-a-half inches.

"You will never play baseball again," Dr. Ryan assured me, as he stared down at my form wilting on the gurney. "It's physically impossible. It can't be done. You might play golf one day. You might toss the ball with your kids in the yard. But you will never, ever pitch again."

I later learned that Dr. Ryan kept that bone spur in a jar in his office for years as a memento.

Eventually, days become years and dreams become memories. That process seems to accelerate when you get news like that. I put baseball out of my mind as best I could and focused on building a life. Our son Hunter was born in 1990. Jessica came into the world in 1994. I graduated from Angelo State and immediately put my energies into teaching and coaching, a natural career path for me.

I eventually did what most teachers and coaches do: I worried about paying the bills and projected my dreams onto the students I taught and the players I coached at Reagan County High School in Big Lake, Texas. I chased those dreams with passion, convinced it was my God-given purpose. I loved watching students' eyes light up when they suddenly grasped a new concept. Getting out on the baseball field to mentor and stoke passions for this game I love, in the next generation of players, was exhilarating.

The capstone moment was a bet I made with my players after they suffered humiliating losses the first two games of my second season as coach. If they won a district championship, I promised, I would honor them by trying out for a Major League Baseball team.

Pitching speed is one of those universal mysteries. Some have it; some don't. You can teach control and technique, but not speed. Speed is something you're born with. Maybe it has something to do with loose joints, or the flexibility of the ligament, tendon, and muscle structure of the wrist, elbow, and shoulder. I don't know. What I do know is that if you consistently throw 88 miles per hour, it's highly unlikely you will ever reach 94.

At the age of twenty-four, as my minor league career ran out of steam, the best I could throw a baseball was in the 87 to 89 mile an hour range—maybe 90 with a lucky release. So, how was I able to—at the age of thirty-five—throw 94, 98, even 102 miles per hour with a shoulder that had most of its animating substance hacked away? The only explanation I have is divine intervention.

∽∾

After the Tampa Bay Devil Rays signed me, they sent me to Rehab Camp in St. Petersburg, Florida. This was where they sent players who were getting over injuries and surgeries. They sent me there to lose the weight I'd gained from too many homemade tortillas and Famous Amos cookies. I thought I was there to pitch. They thought I was there to train for a marathon. They had me running everywhere.

Three weeks later and thirty pounds lighter, they sent me to join the Orlando Rays, the club's AA team, on the road. The Rays were in Zebulon, North Carolina to play the Carolina Mudcats. As soon as I got there, I headed straight for the clubhouse.

"Hey, we got a new coach," one of the players said.

People always ask me what it was like playing with kids who were barely older than the kids I was coaching. I discovered the answer here. My first night with the team, they put me in the game and I struck out a batter unleashing pitches at 91 and 92 miles per hour.

"Hey, he's not crazy. He's pretty good for an old guy," they said.

On the second night I threw two innings, striking out five batters throwing pitches between 98 and 99 miles per hour. I also learned that there is a vast difference in maturity level between nineteen years of age and thirty-five.

On the bus ride back to the hotel, those young players started asking me questions.

"Are you married?"

"Yes." I told them my wife's name and what she did.

"Do you have any kids?"

"Yes. I have three." I told them their names and ages.

Then someone piped up from the back of bus, a player who I didn't even realize was part of the conversation.

"So, after each kid, did you start throwing harder?" He asked.

"Why, yes I did. And I'm gonna have a couple more."

After my experience with the AA team, I went and played for the AAA Durham Bulls for the next eight weeks. AAA is the next to the best level of baseball in the world; in AAA, you're just a phone call away from the big leagues. I had never been that close to Major League Baseball in my life. And now, because of a group of high school kids, I was on the cusp of my dreams.

My players were watching everything I did through Internet feeds. They saw every game I pitched for the Bulls. The computer teacher at Reagan County High—who detested me because I was a coach and coaches don't know how to teach—now had her classroom open for my players every night to watch me pitch. I wasn't making decisions on the field anymore. *I* was a decision.

Over those eight weeks with the Bulls, I got better and better. Still, as the season progressed, I doubted I would get called up—which was okay. I still had the opportunity to go back and coach football and baseball for a school in Fort Worth.

I made friends with another pitcher during my stint with the Bulls. His name was Bobby Muñoz, formerly with the Baltimore Orioles, and he was trying to get back on the mound in the big leagues after elbow surgery. I was the eighth inning pitcher; he was our ninth inning closer. We spent time together in the bullpen every night. If it turned out we didn't get called up to the Majors, we had plans to drive back to Texas together.

On the last night of the season, we faced the Charlotte Knights. We were down 2 to 1 when I scaled the mound in the eighth inning, and down by the same score when Muñoz came off the mound in the ninth. Our AAA season was over. It was time to go home.

We were at our lockers discussing which route we would take back to Texas when the manager came up behind me and tapped me on the shoulder.

"I need to talk to you," he said. I looked around the locker room and then looked back at the manager.

"I don't think so," I said. "The last six guys you talked to are all crying right now."

He just gave me a look, so I followed him to his office. I had my head down, but it wasn't because I was sad or upset. I was just trying to process everything I'd been through in the last three months. I'd gone from grading papers for students uninterested in the notes I'd written on them, to people scrambling to get my autograph.

"You can smile," the manager said once we got to his office. "You're going to be in Texas tomorrow."

"I know," I said. "Bobby and I are headed there right now."

"The Devil Rays are in Arlington playing the Rangers," he said. "There's a big league uniform there waiting on you."

I stepped back. *You have to be kidding me,* I thought. When I tried to chase my dream by myself, for myself, it never worked. When I tried to do it for someone else, everything fell into place. I pushed those kids as hard as I could. They pushed back. We both became successful.

⁓◌⁓

In Anaheim, in 1999, I did an ESPN interview with Rob Dibble, a right-hander who was World Series Champion and National League Series Most Valuable Player with the 1990 Cincinnati Reds.

"Gotten hazed yet?" he asked.

"No Rob, I haven't gotten hazed yet."

That night I had a great outing pitching two scoreless innings against the Angels, who dominated us by a score of 8 to 5. Though we lost, I felt really good about my performance. After the game, I went into the locker room. I discovered that all my clothes were gone. My bags were gone. In their place was a skirt that hit just above the knee, a bra, a blouse, a wig, some high-heeled shoes, and a thong. "Ring My Bell," was stitched into the fabric.

I was the schoolmarm. *Thank God I got that skirt,* I thought. All of the other rookies—who were substantially younger than I was—had to wear miniskirts.

I wore that ensemble all the way from Anaheim to New York. But at the same time that we were making our way to the Big Apple, President Clinton had flown into town. That added two hours to our five-hour cross-country trek, circling the city, waiting for clearance to land.

I do not know how anyone can possibly wear a thong. I was perfectly miserable in that horrid outfit. At 8 a.m., I stepped off the bus in downtown Manhattan and wanted to do nothing more than sleep.

"Look at the freaks coming into town," one of the locals said after taking a look at my getup.

Right next to that guy was another person holding a poster of me pitching in Anaheim the night before. I knew baseball fans could be rabid—they live, eat, and breathe the game all season long. But I never imagined what it was like to live with these fan passions as a ballplayer.

Unfortunately, my teammates thought it was best I not get my clothes back until half an hour before we made our way from the hotel to the stadium. There was a knock on my door and when I opened it, the athletic trainer was standing there holding my bag.

I hustled to get dressed. Rays right hander and my friend, Roberto Hernandez (Bert), was waiting on me.

"How'd that thong feel?" he greeted me.

"How do you think it felt?"

The next day, our game against the Yankees was rained out. Devil Rays' first baseman Fred McGriff took a dozen of us out to an Asian restaurant for dinner and covered the whole bill. I can't begin to fathom what that meal cost. In my mind, I was still living on a teacher's salary. We stayed at the bar eating and drinking until the place closed at 2 a.m. and I went to my room and collapsed.

At 6 a.m., I got a wake-up call from Bert.

"Be downstairs in an hour and a half," he said.

At 7:30 a.m. Bert and a couple of other Devil Rays team-mates escorted all of us rookies down a Manhattan street to a men's clothing store. When we arrived, Bert reached through the pulled down wrought iron bars and knocked on the window. Immediately, the storeowner opened the shop. All the rookies were treated to new shirts, shoes, suits, and ties, all custom fit. After that night's game, I found all of my new clothes had been delivered and hung in my hotel room closet.

I was completely flabbergasted. Teammates do nice stuff like that for each other all the time, though it's rare that you hear or read about it.

In my short Major League career, I pitched fifteen innings in twenty-one games. I had thirteen strikeouts, ten walks, one hit by pitch, and one wild pitch. I gave up two home runs.

My record stands at zero wins, zero losses, and zero saves.

But what I remember most about the game was not that short list of stats. It's the camaraderie. I missed being part of a team that lived and played together and supported each other in an intensely competitive environment. I mourned that this Frankenstein body couldn't keep playing the greatest game there ever was.

CHAPTER 4

THE BIG SCREEN

Fame hit me like a broken bat line drive when I went into AAA baseball. TV news magazines like *20/20* and *48 Hours*, in addition to other media outlets, were calling me for interviews every single day. "Who's the old guy who was coaching a group of kids and is now back trying to play baseball at thirty-five years old? At first people thought it was kind of funny. And then more people interviewed me.

I felt sorry for the girl who did PR for the Durham Bulls. She would meet us at the front gate every day when I'd come in for batting practice. She'd say, "Okay, before stretching you have this interview. After stretching you have that interview. After batting practice you have this one, and before the game you have that one." A month into my AAA stint, boom microphones were crowding me in the bullpen and people were trying to listen to every word we said. It generated all of this momentum, but in the end I was just a little bitty coach from this itty-bitty West Texas town who made a bet with his baseball team.

One of my first roommates in minor league baseball back in the early 1980s was Mark Ciardi. He was a pitcher with a great breaking ball, and he ended up playing for the Milwaukee Brewers in 1987. But he quit baseball and headed for Europe to pursue a modeling career. Mark eventually made his way to Hollywood to get into the movie business and became a successful producer of such films such as *Invincible*, *Secretariat*, *Million Dollar Arm*, and *Chappaquiddick*.

Mark regularly worked out with Michael Eisner, then CEO of the Walt Disney Company. One day as they were doing their routines during their lunch hour, they saw a TV interview with me in Durham. Mark called me that day.

"We were talking at lunch, and we may want to do a movie about you," he said. "Get out of here!" I snapped back. "I haven't heard from you in fifteen years. No, that's not happening."

But he kept calling. So, I said to my agent, Steve Canter, "Make this guy go away."

Everything hit DEFCON 1 when I got called up to the big leagues. After I'd pitched in my Major League debut that Thursday night in Texas, we had an afternoon game the next day. We flew to Anaheim, California for a series with the Angels the following Saturday evening. Sports journalist Bill Plaschke had interviewed all of my high school kids and published an article in the Sunday *Los Angeles Times*. They had to change my name at the hotel where I was staying because of the media frenzy. There were calls coming in to the clubhouse—to veteran players—hoping to reach me or my agent at the hotel. People were proposing books, documentaries, and feature films.

I was a guest on *60 Minutes*, *CBS This Morning*, and a host of other news and entertainment shows. The passionate interest in my story really perplexed me. I was just this fat old dude doing this thing with this group of kids. *This isn't going anywhere*, I'd thought. *You will just go out there and try out. You will go to the minors.* I never thought it would go any further than that. But it was all going so fast and I was so busy living it, I didn't have time to reflect. It was just a part of the game.

Over the course of the next few days in Anaheim, we met with a bunch of production companies. We had meetings with Universal, Paramount, and actor Noah Wyle's production company among others. Each wanted to put their individual spin on the story. One wanted to put the goings-on inside the clubhouse, the mistresses, drugs, steroids—you name it. Another wanted to throw a woman in here, an extramarital affair in there.

"Dude, that is not what this is about," I responded with irritation. I was really getting sick of the whole process. It got to the point where we would walk into a meeting, a guy would start to say something, and I would look at Steve and get up and walk out.

Disney was our last appointment. As we were walking across the Walt Disney studio grounds in Burbank, Steve looked at me and asked, "What do you want out of your movie?"

"I want a movie about kids who have been counted out," I said, "kids who get a chance they never thought would come their way to do something they never thought they could ever do. I want a movie about adults getting a second chance and going for something they thought was long gone, achieving the dream they thought was dead."

And we went in and sat down with the people from Disney, and the producer looks at me and says, "What we had in mind is a movie about kids who..." and he repeated exactly what I had said walking across the grounds. "Oh, my God," I said to Steve. "They have microphones everywhere." I was sold when we walked out.

The story just kept gaining momentum. I was stunned by the A-list actors who wanted to play me: Jim Caviezel, Aaron Eckhart, and Matthew McConaughey, among others.

Not long after the movie came out, I met Jim Caviezel and his wife on an airplane while making a connection in Buffalo. I was on my way to the Baseball Hall of Fame in Cooperstown, New York.

"I almost got to play you," he said.

Two years later, Caviezel played Jesus in *The Passion of the Christ*. If you're going to have an actor play you in a Hollywood movie, that's the dude to do it.

Even Denzel Washington considered the starring role in *The Rookie* at one point. "Hey, we know he's right-handed, but we can put up mirrors and make him look left-handed," the producers said.

"You guys think of everything," I replied.

⸎

John Lee Hancock directed *The Rookie*. He produced *My Dog Skip*, and wrote the screenplay for *Midnight in the Garden of Good and Evil*. He went on to direct *The Blind Side*, *The Alamo*, and *Saving Mr. Banks*. Dennis Quaid said he had been calling Disney since he'd heard about *The Rookie*. The film was a big break for Mark Ciardi, too. I look back now and think, wow, that movie was a breakthrough for a lot of people.

Rachel Griffiths (*My Best Friend's Wedding, Hilary and Jackie, Saving Mr. Banks*), who played my ex-wife Lorri, blew my mind when I met her. She was doing a scene and talking like a West Texas redneck and, after the director yelled "cut," she walked over to me and hugged me around the neck. She started speaking to me in her thick Australian accent.

"Are you the same person who was just talking?" I asked. She laughed at me.

I didn't even know who Scottish actor Brian Cox was. I walked in one night when they were filming a scene at the ballpark, and when he finished everyone gave him a standing ovation.

"Who's that guy?" I asked Mark.

"That's Brian Cox, man," he says. "He's playing your dad."

I went home and it seemed like the next sixty movies I saw had Brian Cox in them, most famously *The Bourne Identity, Rise of the Planet of the Apes, Braveheart,* and *Troy.* He's very good. He either makes you like him or hate his guts.

People in Hollywood like to talk about how normal they are. And if you consider being catered to for every whim, having every opinion you have taken seriously, and having everyone agree with everything you have ever said, than yeah, they're normal. Hollywood likes to say that they march to the beat of their own drum. But all they're really trying to do is stay relevant and popular in any given moment.

They're always trying to prove something to somebody. If they don't think they're getting the press they deserve, they'll say something controversial to get their name in the headlines. And they'll stick with that statement no matter what because if they back down, it makes them a liar. They're big children living on a different planet.

I got a good taste of that. Disney gave Dennis Quaid and me the use of their Gulfstream GV jet to travel around the country to do screenings for a three-week publicity tour. The objective was to make sure adults were exposed to the movie because it was rated G. We hit Boston, New York, Washington, D.C., Seattle, San Francisco, Phoenix, Dallas, and Houston, among other major cities.

The crew would ask, "What would you like to eat when you get back on the plane?"

If you were in Seattle, you would order Pacific seafood. If you were in Boston, they served Atlantic seafood. If you were in the South or the Southwest, you'd get Mexican food or barbecue. We could have requested seaweed from Mars, and they would have found a way to get it and it would be there waiting for us when we returned.

The jet was luxurious. Mickey Mouse was imprinted on the back of the plush leather seats. Everything was embroidered with Mickey Mouse ears. Even the glasses were etched with Mickey's ears.

And, I'll admit that when you're treated like that, it's easy to get accustomed to it, and if you're not firmly implanted with your morals and values you think you deserve this luxury on a regular basis. It's really easy to get sucked into that mess.

Dennis and I got along fantastically, though there were days where he didn't feel like getting involved in all of the publicity. He would separate and go off by himself. But if I got too much attention, he suddenly wanted to get involved again. Sometimes he just needed a breather. Sometimes I needed a breather. We had a great time together. While we were filming, we'd go into Austin at night and Dennis would play guitar and sing with his band, *the Sharks*, in one of the bars downtown. The next day, we'd be up before daylight and at the movie set for that day's filming. Hollywood works hard and plays hard.

Thorndale High School, just outside of Austin, was where we filmed all of the scenes set in Big Lake where I coached the high school baseball team. The interior and exterior as well as its baseball field were used to depict Reagan County High School's campus. Thrall High School in Thrall, Texas and its baseball field were used as the setting for Big Lake "away" games.

The Durham Bulls minor league game scenes were shot at Dell Diamond in Roundrock, and the Major League scenes were filmed at The Ballpark in Arlington. When Dennis Quaid ran out for my big league debut during the seventh inning stretch, he looked and me and asked, "Dude, what if I fall down?"

"Then it 'll be a comedy," I said. "Don't worry."

The sheer number of people who work on a movie set is shocking. There are people carrying wires and props. There are people who do nothing but keep records, writing everything down that every person says, and people taking still shots to document every single thing.

They detailed all of the food that was on the set and noted every reporter who was there. They collected every bit of information that they could possibly have on each reporter, so that they would know when, where, and how an article would see print, or where and when a report would hit the airwaves. They trained the opposing team that faced my team. A trainer would come in and do specific baseball workouts to instruct these guys on how to do what they were supposed to do, and when they were supposed to do it.

They had people upon people upon people. It's like a movable army. And they move everything to each location. It all gets kept in order, somehow, and people stick with it in a way that I can't even fathom. My mind doesn't work like that.

They can make something small and insignificant look fantastic. When you're on the set, it looks really humdrum. We shot one scene with the pitcher and the catcher with this massive complex of cameras, chairs, filters, lighting contraptions, and sound equipment on the baseball diamond right behind the mound. But, in the film, all of that stuff disappears and all you see is the pitcher and the catcher.

When Dennis was giving my speech to the high school team kids, the wind was gusting at speeds close to forty-five miles per hour. They had to adjust the camera angle hundreds of times because the wind was blowing and the sun kept changing. They had to swap out filters to keep the lighting consistent. It took twelve hours to shoot just two minutes of film. But in the movie, you couldn't even tell there was a breeze.

Dennis often would ask me what I would say to the team in a particular instance and how I would say it. And then, after not writing anything down, he would go back and repeat word-for-word what I had told him. He would tell me that if I ever saw anything being filmed that I didn't like or that didn't seem true, to tell him about it. And he was true to his word. A lot of the dialogue in *The Rookie* was the result of our actual conversations between takes.

When he wasn't working a scene, Dennis would often be in the outfield with his pitching wedge—taking shots, smoking cigarettes, and hanging out. Then, after changing camera angles, they would announce they were going to shoot again. He'd put his golf club down, film the scene, and they'd look at it again. If they didn't like it, they'd change the camera angle yet again and he would come back. It was like that over and over. I walked away thinking, *this is not glamorous in any way whatsoever!* I was bored out of my skull.

When I go to the movies and watch what unfolds on the screen, I often think, *wow, that's spectacular.* But you don't think about all of the time, effort, and details that go into creating that experience. Every movie I went to after that, for the next few years, would leave me wondering where they had the camera in this scene, or how they got the angle on that. It makes you look at things differently.

⁘

We filmed *The Rookie* in four-and-a-half months, and it took six months to edit. The film had a quick turnaround because they wanted to get it out as close to the actual events as possible. And they left a lot of footage on the cutting room floor.

After filming at night, we would go to a bar that was closed to regular customers. The Hollywood people would come in, have drinks, and watch the dailies—the raw, unedited footage they shot that day. If they liked it, they kept it to be viewed later. If they didn't like what they saw, that's the scene they started with the next morning.

For the scenes at the Ballpark at Arlington recreating my Major League pitching debut, they made announcements during actual Texas Rangers games, inviting fans to hang around after the last inning to take part in the filming. Major League Baseball was fully on board. We filmed for three days, both during the games and after. The producers arranged to give the fans sack lunches and they often stayed until three or four o'clock in the morning just to be a part of the film. Dennis would play golf the next morning, and I would sleep.

Likewise, all of the writers in the press box were actual sports reporters who stayed after the game so that they could be a part of this Disney baseball drama. To fill the seats vacated by fans that wouldn't or couldn't stay, they used cardboard cutouts of people. When I looked out over the crowd in the stands, I couldn't even tell. I was absolutely shocked.

They would film one section of the stadium at a time so that it would look like it was full. When they changed camera angles, runners would go into the stands and move people and the cardboard cutouts to another section of the stadium to fill the seats. Everything was timed down to the second. In the end, they probably had twenty-seven hours of footage for a feature film they whittled down to two hours.

People often ask me what the difference was between the events as they actually happened and how they were portrayed in the movie. In real life, when I faced All-Star Texas Rangers shortstop Royce Clayton, I had him down two strikes on the first two pitches. He fouled off the third pitch over the first base dugout. I finished him off on the fourth pitch.

On the movie set, we tried for eight straight hours one day to get the actor to foul the ball off on that third pitch. It was all for naught. Finally, in frustration, director John Lee Hancock looked at me and said, "You know what? You struck him out in three pitches." And that was a wrap.

When the filming was completed, they brought us to Hollywood to view the rough cut. They wanted us to give them feedback. It was three hours long, in black and white, and there was no musical soundtrack, so there were sound gaps throughout. I thought it sucked.

A month later, I was in Nashville for the annual National Religious Broadcasters Convention. I was invited to speak to the broadcasters following a screening of the final cut. In the span of one month, the film went from more than three hours to two hours and two minutes. I went from disappointed, thinking "this is not what I wanted," to trying to stop myself from crying after viewing it so that I could to speak to these people about what they had just seen. I was blown away.

This group of kids got to have their story told, in a way that never would have been told otherwise. For adults, it was inspiring. It let them know that whatever dream they may have given up on, there is always a second chance.

When *The Rookie* was released, my son Hunter and I were invited to a screening at the White House of President George W. Bush (43). President Bush has always loved baseball. Unfortunately, I had a speaking engagement across the country the same day. I sent my apologies to the president.

Later that month, we were invited again to the White House, this time for a tee ball event on the White House lawn. My agent Steve, Hunter, and I all went. We met and sat with the president and first lady. Cal Ripken was running the game and there were a lot of kids playing and adults watching.

In the second inning of the game, Ripken called me out of the stands to coach. I tried to take everything in: my son sitting in the stands talking to the president and first lady (I'm sure Hunter was entertaining them), me working with Hall of Famer Cal Ripken, and the kids competing on the White House lawn playing my favorite game. Baseball has seen us through most of our country's history, even through the 9/11 terrorist attacks. For a brief moment, politics took a back seat. How refreshing.

After the game, the president—a man who was also a managing general partner of the Texas Rangers in the 1990s, and who threw out one of the most memorable first pitches in baseball history during the World Series at Yankee Stadium in 2001—looked at my ten-year-old son and asked, "Hunter, are you going to be a Major League ballplayer like your dad?"

"No, sir. Baseball sucks," my son snapped back.

I was mortified. Well, not completely: at least he said "sir." So…there's that. Baseball most certainly does not suck. It's the sport that has defined America, time and again.

Baseball teaches us so many of life's greatest lessons: what it means to be a good teammate, how to persevere and not give up, and how to spit sunflower seeds for both distance and accuracy.

"I am not going to be a baseball player," my son continued. "I am going to be a lawyer."

What ten-year-old boy wants to be a lawyer? What movie or TV show could he have possibly seen that would have made studying and practicing law appear half as exciting as surviving forty surgeries for the opportunity to throw a ball 100 miles per hour and have it hit 500-feet in the opposite direction?

Hunter is now, in fact, a lawyer. He chased and realized his dreams in a completely different way than I did. Although there's no movie about it. Yet.

I took my mother to see *The Rookie* in New York. I took my family to see it in Plano, Texas. At one point during the showing with my family, my four-year-old daughter Jaimee stood up on my wife Shawna's lap and yelled, "That's my daddy!" The theater erupted in giggles.

Baseball had been my dream since I was five years old. I ended up in the majors only after being prodded by a group of kids to try out, long after doctors had told me I would never play again. I look back on it now and think: "Did that really happen?" It was just so surreal. I went from coaching baseball in a little town in West Texas, to pitching in the big leagues. And then there's a book and a movie and—oh my God—Disney did the movie. Did that really happen? There was just so much irresistible momentum. I was swept away, trying to survive the process and stay above water.

The publicity tour to promote the film was highly amusing. I remember one instance where Dennis and I went into an interview on a popular entertainment television news show and the host looked dead straight at Dennis and asked him what it was like starring in the *National Lampoon's Vacation* movies. "I think you're thinking of my brother, Randy," Dennis replied. His publicist stood up and said, "That's it. The interview's over." We got up and walked out.

The night, *The Rookie* captured the 2002 ESPY award for Best Sports Movie presented by ESPN. We rode to the Kodak Theater in Los Angeles in a long black limousine that had no air conditioning. A heat wave had hit LA, and we were dressed to the hilt. But we did have warm Capri Sun fruit drinks.

We shared the limo with pro football Hall of Fame running back Eric Dickerson. Nice guy. We saw boxer Muhammad Ali, tennis stars Serena and Venus Williams, actors David Spade and Matthew Perry, Olympic gold medalist Bruce Jenner, Yankees shortstop Derek Jeter, Patriots quarterback Tom Brady, and golf legend Tiger Woods, among many more notables.

After the ESPY was announced, Dennis and I mounted the stage to receive the award. Dennis handed off the ESPY to me. He wanted me to have it. He kept the envelope.

Fourteen years later, in November of 2016, Dennis and I met up at Texas Motor Speedway. He was the Grand Marshall for the NASCAR Cup Series race that weekend. We had just concluded a Jim "The Rookie" Morris Foundation event in Fort Worth to raise money for youth sports programs. Michael McDowell, driver of the #95 Chevrolet, had helped me earlier with a "Meet Me on the Mound" softball game. We brought a group of high school kids to watch McDowell race.

It suddenly hit me that I should give Dennis the ESPY award after all those years. I presented it to him during a press conference. He was shocked, but graciously accepted it.

"I tell you what, I will give it back to you in fourteen years," he said. "How about that?"

After the 2002 awards event at the Kodak, Dennis and I were sent to different parties. As we left the theater, Dennis gave me a hug.

"Man, I just want you to know. You helped turn my career around," he said to me. After everything that had happened—the book, the movie, and all of the accolades—those few words meant a lot to me.

Before *The Rookie*, his career had sunk almost off the charts. He was getting older and Hollywood producers didn't know how to cast him. But after the success of *The Rookie*, the offers started pouring in. It was a resurrection of sorts for him. Hollywood discovered he was versatile and relevant, and all of a sudden he was back in the game.

Sixteen years after playing me in *The Rookie*, Dennis got a role in *I Can Only Imagine*, a solid 2018 box office success. *I Can Only Imagine* was based on the story behind the song of the same name—the best-selling Christian single of all time by the band *MercyMe*. Dennis played *MercyMe* lead singer Bart Millard's abusive father. The character Dennis portrayed, and the mistreatment he unleashed on his son, was exactly like that of my dad. Except I couldn't sing.

CHAPTER 5

DREAM KILLERS

People have different names for those who seem to take pleasure in torpedoing your aspirations. I call them dream killers. These are people who want to see you fail for any number of reasons. I've boiled it down to one of two: 1) they've tried to accomplish something in their life and they've failed, and so they want to tear you down so that you don't show them up; or 2) they're too afraid to take a chance to even try to achieve their dream, and they want to drag you down so that they don't have to face up to their regrets and lack of courage.

Since they believe there's no point in trying, they don't want you to try and expose them as failures. So, they tell you how impossible it is to achieve your dreams. Dream killers delight in failure. They actually want to see you fail, and will sometimes actively work toward that outcome, attempting to undermine every step you take toward actualizing your aspirations.

Dream killers don't have the stamina to do the work necessary to succeed. They give up as soon as the going gets tough. Naturally, they want to see you fail because it makes them more comfortable in whatever situation they find themselves.

My high school guidance counselor was the consummate dream killer. I took my SAT test the morning after we won the state football championship in 1981 against Willowridge High School in Houston, Texas. That team's star player was future NFL Hall of Fame running back Thurman Thomas. After the game and some celebration, we got home at 3 a.m. I got up at six to take the test.

About a third of the way through the test, as I struggled to keep my eyes open and my brain focused, I recalled a saying I'd heard somewhere: "Those who choose 'C' in multiple-choice tests are correct fifty percent of the time." So I played the odds and chose "C" for every remaining multiple-choice question.

That saying was stuck on stupid. I bombed the test. Bad. When my score came back, my counselor stopped me in the hallway.

"Jimmy, what are you going to do with your life?" he asked.

"I'm going to be a baseball player," I said confidently. "Everybody knows that."

"I hope so," he snapped back. "Because you're too stupid to go to college."

What kind of a counselor goes around telling kids they're never going to succeed in college? Isn't it their job to encourage kids to prepare for college, or at least pursue a career track that will lead to success? Counselors are trained to be empathetic and sympathetic. I was blessed with a counselor who was simply pathetic.

I'll be honest: school did not come naturally to me. I found it boring and there were other things I would much rather be doing. But I got the last laugh. I eventually did go to college, and I earned straight A's. Two of my professors even urged me to go to medical school.

After my brief period in the Major Leagues, I heard that counselor no longer worked with kids. That is, unless it was helping them pick out movies to watch at home. He worked in a movie rental store—no doubt renting the film about my life to other people.

Dream killers come in all shapes and forms. They can work at any company doing any job. Dream killers are sometimes people who are—or were once—dream makers.

Gordon Wood, head football coach at Brownwood High School, was one of the most important dream makers in my life. But he was also a dream killer. Shortly after that conversation with my counselor, Coach Wood stopped me in the hallway.

"Jimmy, you've got sixty scholarships to Division I schools to play football," he said. "Son, you're a football player. You're never, ever going to be good enough to play baseball. Give it up now."

I was eighteen. Eighteen-year-olds know everything. Eighteen-year-olds are well-seasoned by life. They've experienced the ups and downs of good and bad grades, and acceptance along with lots of rejection from girls. Eighteen-year-olds are full of wisdom.

"I'm playing baseball and there's absolutely nothing you can do about it," I blurted boldly.

That's how smart I was at eighteen. I pitted my wits against a man who had coached football for thirty-seven years and set state and national records for the most wins, a record that included nine state championships.

"Jimmy, listen closely," he said. "They are giving you scholarships to play *football* at top ranked schools. You'll have tutors who will help you with your classwork and make sure you succeed scholastically. If you go to college to play football, you can punch a ticket straight to the NFL. Son, football is your future."

"I'm playing baseball and that's the end of that," I smarted off.

Two days later, I found out how smart I really was, and the devious lengths Coach Wood would go to in his effort to kill my dream. He called every school—Notre Dame, USC, Arkansas, Penn State, UCLA—and urged them to rescind their scholarship offers because my real ambition was to play baseball. He bragged to me about doing this.

He was essentially saying, "If you're not going to concentrate on the sport that I love, you're not going to play the sport that you love. No grades. No scholarships. You have nowhere to go."

I firmly believe that Coach Wood had it in for me. My dad, an enormously talented athlete, had played football under Coach Wood at Brownwood. He lasted for just two weeks. At the end of that period, when coaches start expecting more out of their players—when practices get long and brutal—my dad quit. Thanks to his shining example, Coach Wood expected me to follow in his footsteps and give up. Like father, like son. So, he was looking to stick it to me in any way possible. The fact that Coach Wood hated baseball didn't help my case any.

Years later, as a consolation of sorts, Wood mentioned me in the book he wrote just before he died: *Coach of the Century, an Autobiography.* He wrote that I was the greatest athlete he had ever coached. He said I had the talent to play any position I so desired. But because I always wanted to make the team better, I did whatever coaches asked me to do.

But I believe the only reason he mentioned me in that book was because of my own success. I made it into the Majors, had a book written about me, and a Hollywood movie produced chronicling my unlikely path into professional baseball. Otherwise, I doubt he would have ever mentioned me at all. His distaste for my father ran far too deep.

∞

The next dream killer in my life was Scott Simpson, the high school athletic director and head football coach at Reagan County High School. The ironic thing about my experience with Simpson is that in his efforts to ruin me, he ended up making me bigger, stronger, and better.

I coached and taught at Reagan County High School for just two years. The baseball team had won a grand total of just one game in each of the three seasons before I got there. During my first year as coach, the team racked up ten wins. The next year, they won the district championship and went to the area playoffs.

But Simpson constantly berated me. I don't know if he was jealous of my success, envious of the rapport I had developed with my players, or just simply couldn't stand me personally. But he was constantly haranguing me. Nothing satisfied him. And every criticism he directed towards me was loud and public.

"You know why I get on you, don't you?" Simpson asked one afternoon after football practice. "It's because the kids like you so much. You're too nice. Kids don't respect that."

As I was preparing the baseball diamond just before the start of my first baseball season, I noticed that much of the equipment I needed to complete the job was locked away in sheds. No one seemed to have the keys, and my requisition requests mysteriously got lost before they could be filled. I confronted Simpson, threatening to take my complaints to the school board. He told me I didn't know what kind of trouble I was making for myself and that I had blinders on.

"You only see small things, not big problems," he said.

"I've learned to tackle big problems by solving small problems," I replied.

Our squabbling got so bad that he challenged me to a fistfight in front of my team. He suggested the spectacle would be good for the players and boost morale. The kids would have a good time. I thought his suggestion was idiotic. I declined.

But Simpson eventually got the best of me: he got me fired. After we won the district championship, my players were drinking beer in the back of the bus during our trip home. They had hidden it in their backpacks. I found out about it when we got back to school after I discovered a beer can in the back of the bus.

I was going to discipline the kids myself, but Simpson took it to the superintendent before I could rebuke them. He accused me of supplying the beer to my players.

"What happened?" the superintendent asked.

"I'm in charge," I replied. "This happened on my watch. Do what you're going to do."

And he did. He fired me. But the truth is, Simpson had been interviewing my coaching replacement long before the district championship game. He even brought candidates into my classroom while I was working with my students to show them the classes they would be teaching. The beer incident was just a way to ensure I was out of the way.

I received a letter from the president of the Reagan County Independent School District school board outlining the divisiveness between me and the athletic director and his unfair attacks on my reputation. The board suggested I use this letter as a character reference with other schools. Thankfully, I didn't have to; I had a new teaching and coaching job within twenty-four hours.

It's hard to fathom the deep and enduring hostility Simpson had for me. My only explanation is that I represented some kind of existential threat to him. The rapport I had with my students and players seemingly undermined his approach and character. The only other person in my life who was so fiercely committed to killing my dreams was my father.

⁓

My father, Jim Morris, was by far the most powerful dream killer in my life. This was odd because he was an incredibly talented man. Built like a tank with an arm like a rocket launcher, he excelled at both football and baseball. My dad's problem was that he was allergic to discipline. He didn't want to work hard to develop and control his outsized talents.

In short: he was lazy. That's why he had frustrated Brownwood coach Gordon Wood. He missed playing on the team Wood built during his first season, the team that brought home the school's first state championship trophy. But my dad had no regrets. He would rather drink, smoke, chase girls, and raise hell than play with champions. Wood always held a grudge against people who gratuitously wasted their talents.

But it wasn't only in athletics that my dad let his laziness get the best of him. He was a musical talent as well, a silky tenor. He had one of the best voices I had ever heard, and he sang in the church choir and would sometimes perform solos during services. For some strange reason, his choir teacher at Brownwood High School was able to get through to him. She got him to study and practice to the point that he could sight sing sheet music, and he was an all-state choral performer.

But he never took it further. He just didn't care.

My father was also, without a doubt, the smartest person I have ever known. He could do math problems in his head that would take me two or three pages of scrawled calculations to solve. His academic chops were so sharp he was able to qualify for Nuclear Power School, a technical institute operated by the U.S. Navy. "Nuke school," as it was called, trained enlisted sailors and officers on the operation and maintenance of nuclear surface ships and submarines. To break into this elite academy, enrollees must pass the Armed Services Vocational Aptitude Battery, the nuclear aptitude test, and undergo an investigation to attain a Secret security clearance. My dad cleared all of these hurdles, only to get kicked out because he didn't want to abide by Navy rules. He always found a way to sabotage his own success.

But that was his M.O. He was always itching for a fight, always looking to break the rules. Or someone's jaw. He would hit somebody during a game of baseball or football just so he could exchange blows. That's why we moved around so much while he was in the navy: he was always getting busted for fighting and getting transferred as a result.

With my father, I saw someone who could have done anything he wanted to, but he just hid from life. He wanted to keep his talents to himself, barricaded behind a wall of aggression.

My mother, Olline Ketchum, met my father in Brownwood during the summer of 1962. One hot night, she pulled her car into the Dairy Maid parking lot, one of the town's top hangouts for teens and young adults. At five foot ten, she was graceful, leggy, and blond, with creamy porcelain skin unmolested by the searing West Texas sun. She spotted my father standing next to his car, his wavy black hair sculpted into a flattop. His broad shoulders and muscled arms strained the fabric of his tight T-shirt.

He walked towards her, smiling as he stopped at her car. He folded his arms above her car window and wooed her with small talk. They had a date the next night. Not long after, he left for San Diego and shipped out on a submarine. For the next six months they carried on a torrid romance— via pen, paper, and postage.

He returned to Texas the following April while on leave, and their relationship progressed rapidly. By May, my mother discovered she was pregnant. They married in a minister's house on a steamy hot afternoon in early July. I arrived the following January.

My father never forgave me for that.

"Your brother's the one we wanted," he would say to me, always out of earshot of my mother. "We didn't want you. You're the reason we had to get married."

My father punished me for this over the next fifteen years. That punishment took many forms. There were his words.

"You're not smart enough."

"You're not good enough."

"Why do you even try?"

"Children are to be seen and not heard."

"Why don't you quit now before you embarrass yourself and everybody else?"

He salted his inspiring statements with four letter words and names you wouldn't call anyone, let alone your own child. These are the words that, if you hear them enough, you start to believe. You learn to see yourself through those words.

He also punished me with his actions.

For the first fifteen years of my life, I was a military brat. We moved east, west, north, and south. Each time we pulled up stakes, I lost whatever friends I had made. And there wasn't any texting or social media platforms through which we could connect and maintain friendships. For that first decade-and-a-half of my life, I grew up mostly alone, learning life's lessons from a diehard dream killer.

At one point, after he got busted for starting another fistfight, the Navy put my dad in charge of the recreation hall where brand new pool tables had just been delivered. He brought me to work with him one day just after he got the position. I was four years old.

He sat me down in his office next to several boxes of new billiard balls.

"Do not move," he said. "And do not touch the new pool balls."

But when I was four, balls mesmerized me. I loved the feel of them. I loved rolling them and throwing them. So I pulled one of the colorful balls out of the box and played with it. When my father returned to his office, he was not happy.

"I thought I told you not to play with those fucking balls!" he bellowed. He grabbed a pool cue, jammed it into my stomach, and walked off. That blow knocked the wind out of me. I sat there crying, struggling for several minutes to catch my breath. This was at a time when I suffered from asthma.

A year later, my father and his brother Bob took me out in a boat out on Lake Brownwood to go fishing. We had been living in California at the time, and we went to Brownwood to visit family while my father was on leave.

"My son can't swim worth shit," my father said to my uncle. To prove it, my father grabbed me up and threw me overboard. I struggled for a few seconds before sinking like a bowling ball into the dark waters, flapping my arms and kicking my legs in a desperate attempt to reach the surface. He left me to flounder like that without lifting a finger. That's when my uncle stripped off his shirt dove into the water to rescue me.

When he got me back into the boat, I choked up water trying to recover my breath. My father laughed hysterically, a cruel guffaw that terrified me as much as the water. Due to that trauma, I failed swimming lessons four times over the next few years. But through the sheer force of will, I conquered that fear and ended up teaching myself how to swim. My swimming skills grew so proficient that I eventually became a lifeguard.

My father had a hair-trigger temper, and the smallest things would set him off. Maybe I didn't get all of my chores done. Or maybe I was supposed to be watching my little brother Kael and he screwed something up. Or maybe it was just the mood he was in. I became an expert at reading emotions. I could tell what mood my parents were in simply by the way they got out of the car when they came home from running errands or from some appointment. If I sensed a hostile threat, I would hide in my closet until the emotional storm passed.

One of my father's favorite punishments was popping me in the back of the head with his open palm. But it wasn't his palm flesh that drew the most pain. It was the thick gold ring he wore with a big sparkling ruby in the setting. He would turn that ring around so that the ruby was just above his palm before he swung his hand into my skull. The welts in my head were like trophies to him, at least that's how it seemed.

One evening after my father came home late, he made his way to my room while I was asleep. Something I did that day set him off, and he was going to drag me out of bed and slap me around. But my German Shepherd Nick, who slept at the foot of my bed, attacked him before he could get to me, knocking my dad down the stairs.

The next morning, Nick was gone. My father said he sold him. I'm convinced my dad took him out to a field somewhere and shot him dead.

This incessant abuse continued throughout my childhood, until the day I stood up to him and refused to suffer his attacks in silence. During my freshman year in high school, I had a steady girlfriend—my first real sweetheart. She was an athlete, like me. In fact, I wondered if we could ever have a serious relationship because we were both so consumed with sports.

One day when I came home from practice, my father met me.

"You'd better watch out," he said. "Ants are going to catch that sugar ass of yours."

I didn't even know what that meant.

"Well, at least I'm not fat like you," I shot back.

I walked off. He pursued me with clenched fists. My mother overheard our exchange and watched him come after me. This didn't bother him. He liked an audience when he put me down or physically abused me. I'm sure that's why he threw me into Lake Brownwood in front of his brother. It was performance art in his mind.

"If you touch him, I will kill you," she said. He backed off.

Yet, while she sometimes intervened to thwart his attacks, my mother wasn't above dishing out abuse. She would beat the crap out of me for some small infraction and then afterwards hug me and offer apologies through tears of regret. She was deeply unhappy, but she didn't know how to deal with it.

Right after the incident over my girlfriend, my father left for a year-and-a-half. He supposedly went overseas on some secret mission for the Navy. He once even claimed he was a Navy SEAL, but that was pure bull. While on this "mission," he would occasionally call and talk to my mother and my little brother Kael. But he refused to talk to me. I was fine with that. I was relieved he was gone.

When I turned fifteen, I was playing on the McArthur High School varsity baseball team in Hollywood, Florida. I was the second freshman to ever make the team. The University of Miami, which had a fantastic baseball program, was keeping tabs on my game play, scouting me for a collegiate baseball scholarship. My ambition at that time was to play baseball for Miami before moving on to a professional club after graduation. The yellow brick road leading to stardom was laid out before me.

Two weeks into my first varsity season, my dad came home with a manila envelope. Those envelopes always contained orders.

"Guess what?" he said. "We're moving to Brownwood, Texas."

Brownwood is 1,500 miles west of Hollywood. It had a population of 15,000, a far cry from what I was used to in Florida.

"We're moving to Texas, so you can play football for the same coach I played for when I was in high school," my dad assured me.

Like most teenagers, I was well versed in the art of sarcasm. My mouth often said things before my brain could intervene.

"Is that guy still alive?"

"Yes," he said after I got up off the floor a little dazed.

Everything I had done to become the best baseball player I could be, all the time I put in, all the hard work, meant nothing. The dream was throttled and put on the shelf.

My dad did come to a few of my Brownwood High School football games. He showed up at the quarterfinal, final, and state championship games. But before it really counted, he was AWOL.

Long after that, because I was who I was, he wanted to make sure everyone knew who *he* was. He was always the loudest voice in the stands during my baseball games. I could always pick out his yelling over everybody else. And I hated every second of it.

෩

When you're living with an abusive person and you are completely powerless to defend yourself or make it stop, you use your mind to rationalize the circumstances. To my thinking, if I showed no emotion during these attacks, I was winning these battles with my father.

But I had another motivation: my little brother, Kael, who was six years my junior. I desperately wanted to protect him from the kind of abuse I was experiencing. I can't explain it, but my dad never seemed to direct the same kind of rage at him as he did toward me. I always knew that Kael had been a child they had planned and wanted. I was not.

Like the old adage about kicking the dog to diffuse rage, I had become my father's dog. I think that once the dynamic was established, our parts in this family drama were cast. Maybe the fact that I took it so stoically perpetuated the drama. Maybe he just wanted to break me, and I wouldn't let him. My goal was to withstand anything he could possibly dish out. Like a stereotypical male jock, I dismissed him. "That guy may be my father, but he was never my dad," I said to myself. I didn't want to have anything to do with him after I left home for college.

My mother was also a victim of his fury, even if it manifested differently. I always wondered why she didn't intervene to save us. Her restraint left me insecure and resentful. She later apologized for allowing the family turmoil to get as bad as it did. Who knows what would have happened if she had tried to confront him?

Realistically, we were all captives in an abusive situation, and none of us had a playbook for how to escape, much less win. We were individuals bound together in a struggle driven by someone who probably had diagnosable mental health issues. In the late '60s and '70s, at least where I grew up, people weren't really enlightened about issues surrounding mental health.

We knew no clinical names. We couldn't say, "Oh, dad is bipolar or manic depressive." And, we certainly didn't know that a cocktail of medications could have potentially normalized his life—and ours. We just survived.

Ironically, my dad probably drove me to excel because I was exceedingly easy to coach. I had fear and respect beaten into me, and no coach was ever going to be as bad as what I experienced at home.

Years later, after he and my mother divorced, I tried to have a talk with him, hoping he would express some measure of remorse. He showed no sign of comprehending what I was even talking about, and he certainly didn't feel that he had any reason to apologize. By this time, there was little left in his life. His demons were eating him alive. He weighed just south of 400 pounds and his only companions were his chain-smoking second wife, his more than a dozen cats, Jack Daniels, and Marlboro. In fact, his house was an unmitigated disaster. He had no litter boxes, and the feline urine and feces filled the house with a thick, stinking fog. A sticky layer of soot and tar embedded with clumps of cat hair covered the walls from their incessant smoking.

After my grandfather had died, I talked to my grandmother about my father. "I don't know what happened to him," she said. "I don't know where it went wrong. He's been that way for a long time."

I didn't go to my thirtieth high school reunion. My father spread a rumor that I would only attend if I were paid ten thousand dollars for an appearance in the wake of my Major League Baseball career, the book, and the Disney movie. That rumor circulated around Brownwood.

In fact, the reasons I didn't attend were twofold. One, I wasn't sentimental about high school; and two, I had a conflicting speaking engagement halfway across the globe.

The last time I spoke to my father was at my grandmother's funeral in May of 2016, after she passed away at the age of ninety-six. I approached him and told him how sorry I was that he had lost his mother. He turned to me sitting in the church pew behind him, and sneered.

"Don't ever fucking talk to me again," he said. My father thought the book and the movie were a sham because I made him look bad. He tried to get my mom to sue me for slander.

"It was way worse than that, and you know it," she said to him.

My father died on April 1, 2017. He had a massive heart attack and went into a coma before he succumbed to pneumonia days later. He was seventy-four.

I was in Seattle for a speaking engagement when he died. My uncle Bob called me with the news, just as I was getting ready to go on stage. He told me that the funeral was in a few days, and they were going to wait until I got home to have the service.

I didn't attend the funeral.

My father is buried in Brownwood. I still haven't visited his gravesite. I doubt I ever will. Yes, I have forgiven him, but not because he apologized and asked for my forgiveness. That never came. I chose to forgive him for me. I've learned that forgiveness is something we do for ourselves. Forgiveness is freedom.

⁓

Over the years, I've come to realize that when I married my wife Lorri, I had essentially married a version of my father. It was déjà vu. I believe we both were trying to fix unresolved issues in each other that we had experienced in our past. We had a similarly volatile relationship. It wasn't violent or physically abusive, but there was a lot of passive aggression and undercurrents of contempt between us, fueled by deceit and a lack of intimacy. These problems were magnified by the stresses of raising and providing for three children.

We strived to find common ground but that's hard to do when you're going in different directions. We always agreed that our children were our first priority. Unfortunately, the children became our only priority.

But no matter what we did, we just couldn't connect and resolve our issues. We finally divorced in 2002. The final years of our marriage were filled with loneliness, unhappiness, and hostility, at least from my point of view. Even so, I will always be grateful to Lorri for our three wonderful children who are happy, healthy, and chasing their dreams.

I've had dream killers circling me for virtually my entire life. For some reason, I seem to attract them. But I fought back. I overcame. I found a way to succeed without attacking them in the same manner they came after me. I moved forward by being the best I could be. When someone told me I couldn't do something, I found a way to do it.

If you told me I'm not going to make it in baseball, then I'm going to go play baseball. If Coach Wood had told me I was never ever going to make it in football, I probably would have played football. But because he said I couldn't make it in baseball, that's the direction I chose.

Dream killers are those people who are constantly saying the worst things they can say at the exact point in time you need a word of encouragement. They take delight in destroying hope. They enjoy watching you fail. They simply cannot stand the thought that someone else might succeed.

Most likely, though, dream killers are those people who are too afraid to try. They have tuned into the voice of fear, and believe its lies to be true. They don't have the courage to take the leap, to try out for the team, to never give up when life gets hard. Dream killers want to drag you down to their level, where dreams are little more than regret and longing. Unfortunately, it often seems that there are more dream killers in this world than dream makers. Pay no attention to this disparity.

The most important skill to develop in successfully dealing with dream killers is learning to recognize them. You've got to realize that any attempt to talk to them, reason with them, or persuade them to change will be futile and is likely to boomerang on you. So, you've got to cut this toxicity out of your life like the tumor that it is.

If you work in a company infested with dream killers, find another job. Get transferred to a different office. Do something about it. Distance yourself from dream killers. Then find a place where you can surround yourself with good people—dream makers. There are divisive people everywhere. Your job is to take the high road and do the right thing while searching for the best people to help you reach your dream.

"Why do I always get stuck with toxic people? Why do all of these bad things keep happening to me?" we may ask ourselves. I stopped asking these questions. I no longer ask why I'm having all of these surgeries or why bad things happen to me. Instead, I endure, adapt, and overcome. I pray and trust that God has me. He always has. My problem is that sometimes I forget and think I have to do it all myself.

I learned to look at it through a lens of faith. It's like my grandfather always said: "There are two types of people: good people and bad people." Our job is to surround ourselves with as many good people as we can.

CHAPTER 6

DREAM MAKERS

To attract dream makers, you've got to *be* a dream maker. It doesn't just happen out of the blue. There's a logic to it. Because of my experiences growing up, I developed the ability to discern the moods and states of mind of those around me. I could watch the behavior of my parents as they pulled into the driveway and got out of the car and instantly know if I needed to hide from them. As I adapted to survive in this turbulent environment, I could observe other people and size them up almost instantly, just by how they carried themselves.

That same principle applies here. If you're going to be negative and find ways to downgrade people and sermonize on why they can't achieve their dreams, you're going to repel people; you're going to lose. The people you need to help you achieve your dreams will be able to size you up and disengage from you. To thrive, you need to make yourself more appealing to both those who have succeeded and those who are striving to achieve their dreams. This applies to the people you hang out with, who you enjoy your hobbies with, and who you go to church with. It applies to most everyone and everything.

I didn't get a second chance to play baseball at thirty-five because of anything I did for me. It was because of what I did for other people. I dedicated myself to building up my high school baseball team. In that process, I got my baseball dream back. And achieving that aspiration whet my appetite for my current dream of traveling all over to share my message with others, a dream I never knew I wanted.

That's an interesting turn of events for someone who proclaims he doesn't really like people. Sometimes, I'd rather be without people. I prefer dogs because dogs never let you down. You could have just had the worst day on the planet and be in a miserable mood, but when you walk in your door, that dog is going to be happy to see you.

Whether you play baseball, work in an office, or toil outside in the elements for a telecom company, 95 percent of the people you encounter day in and day out are going to be good people. Don't assume someone is rotten without giving them a fair shake. While about 5 percent of those you run into will be total jerks, most are upstanding people who might happen to be frightened of something. Just be sure to steer clear of those who are clearly toxic. If you don't, they're going to get into your head and poison your outlook—and your chances for success.

But if you find someone, like I found my wife Shawna for example, and surround yourself with likeminded friends and family who nurture and encourage you while embodying a living example of success, you will be lifted. You've got to be able read people. It's pretty easy to sort the gems from the cow-patties.

I have often been asked what my favorite ballpark is, and without hesitation I say Fenway Park in Boston. I've told the story about how, as a ten-year-old little league all-star, my team and I traveled from Connecticut to Boston to watch the Red Sox play the Milwaukee Brewers.

If I could play on that field one day, that would be incredible, I remember thinking to myself.

I sat down at the left field line under the rafters watching the game. Carlton Fisk hit two home runs and almost hit a third out of the park. At that game, I got an autographed ball from my baseball dream maker, Hank Aaron, who then played for the Brewers. It was the season after he broke Babe Ruth's home run record. For the entire game, he did nothing but sign baseballs for my all-star teammates and me. Even at ten, I knew he was a great player. What I found out later made me appreciate his accomplishments even more.

As ball players and military brats, those of us growing up on a base played with whoever wanted to play the game. Color didn't matter. Race didn't matter. As I got older, I began to realize all of the hatred Hank Aaron endured while successfully playing at the highest-level of the game. It struck me as unfathomable. Hank Aaron is an icon.

Have you seen the movie, *The Sandlot?* Where a boy ruins a baseball signed by Babe Ruth? As I relayed in Chapter 3, while living in Connecticut as a boy, we often played in lots of snow. There was a fateful winter day when, while playing baseball, we ran out of balls. We lost or ruined every one of them in the slush and snow.

"Hey, I've got one," I said.

I ran home and got my autographed Hank Aaron baseball. By the time we finished the game two hours later, that ball was completely waterlogged. It weighed about ten pounds. The signature was gone.

I was blessed to pitch at that iconic park twenty-five years after that tragic incident. I ran out on to that same field. I looked out toward the "Green Monster," the park's famous thirty-seven-foot-high left field wall. I got everyone out in my two innings on the mound against the Red Sox. No one smacked one against or over the Green Monster. I was doubly blessed.

Fast forward to the release of *The Rookie*. I had been invited by Russell Athletics to ring the closing bell at the New York Stock Exchange with Hank Aaron. I was in awe standing next to the man. By that time, I knew what he stood for and all that he suffered through to become the greatest home run hitter in the game. I told him the story of watching him at Fenway, and of "sand lot-ing" his signed ball.

"When I was ten years old, you signed a baseball for me. That was incredibly awesome," I said.

He smiled.

"But then one day while playing a game in the winter, we ran out of baseballs. So I took my Hank Aaron ball outside so we could keep playing. It got ruined."

He's listened, laughing a little bit, giving me a look out of the side of his eye.

"Is there any way you'll sign another baseball for me?" I asked. He put his arm around me and laughed really hard.

"I would have if you hadn't told me that story," he said.

I guess sometimes honesty isn't the best policy. At least I have a plaque commemorating the time we were at the stock exchange together:

Jim Morris
100th Anniversary Celebration
Russell Corporation
March 1, 2002
RML
Listed
NYSE

Hammerin' Hank endured death threats and bags of hate mail during the 1973–1974 offseason before he broke Babe Ruth's "sacrosanct" home run record on April 8, 1974 in Atlanta. No one would ever know the true extent of the personal price he paid chasing that record—all because he was a person of color. He is the epitome of a dream maker.

⤜⤛

I've been blessed to have had many dream makers in my life. Among the most significant was Gordon Wood, head coach of the Brownwood High School football team. Now, as I pointed out in Chapter 5, Coach Wood was also a dream killer. But I learned several invaluable lessons from him that I had never learned from anyone else. Coach Wood taught us that it doesn't matter how big, fast, or strong you are. What's most important is the grit, determination, and persistence you have on the inside.

He taught me that you could compete and win if you have a better plan and more heart than your competition. And we won. Consistently. In many of those victories, we were not the most talented team on the field. But we were not going to lose. That possibility never entered our minds.

Coach Wood did not believe that "practice makes perfect." He believed "perfect practice makes perfect." This lesson was easy for us to absorb because we often practiced until 9:00 p.m. We ran through every play, every drill until they were perfected.

Bottom line: we outworked everybody. If it was Monday and Coach Wood came out with a list of plays thirty-five long, we would run through each and every play. If we screwed up on play number thirty-four, we started over at number one. And if we had to run these plays in the dark, by God we were doing them in the dark. Until each and every player knew exactly what he was supposed to be doing. Cold.

We knew before we ever took the field what the other team was going to do before they did. We knew because we studied their maneuvers and practiced our plays until we knew them inside and out. We were acting instead of reacting. If we saw somebody moving one way, we were already moving the other way. So, if the ball is coming right here, I've already got you stopped.

But Coach Wood stoked team involvement from more than just the players and coaches on the football team. He enlisted the whole town of Brownwood. He would host coffee shop meetings and engage with parents, booster clubs, and community organizations. They talked about what went on during the games and what the team was preparing for next week's game.

He was constantly politicking to make sure he had the backing of everyone in Brownwood in his mission to win and transform adolescent football players into strong, ethical men. Everyone was watching his players making sure they stayed on track. Consequently, as far as the town was concerned, Gordon Wood could do no wrong.

Back before game films became such a big deal, competing coaches were supposed to exchange two films from the season so that opposing teams could prepare for the eventual contest. But you couldn't always trust that the films provided accurately reflected the opposing team play-book. So, Coach Wood would recruit teachers and parents to attend games throughout the season—8-millimeter movie cameras in hand—to film the current plays our competition was running.

If we played on Friday night, on Saturday, after all of the players had practiced, the coaches would stay, break down those game films, and draw up plays. They knew who the opposing players were, their numbers, and what their role was in each play. The following Monday, they gave us packets with all of the drawn-up plays so that we knew what we were up against: what the opposing team was going to do, when they were going to do it, and how they would execute. We were prepared every which way but upside down. It's astounding, the level of preparation that went into high school football.

Teamwork is essential to make any dream come true. Over the course of my high school career, Coach Wood taught me how to be a team player. He taught us that the weakest link in the chain will break down your team—and cause you to lose. My senior year, we captured the Texas state football championship and we were definitely not the best team on the field. We were simply the most prepared.

We won through sheer hard work and determination. He made us want to win.

Gordon Wood had a work ethic that was beyond belief. During our awards ceremony at the end of the football season, as the players approached the dais to receive awards, Coach Wood was seated at the front table busily scribbling. He was drawing up plays for the next season with the players he had in mind. On a napkin.

In that way, he was the quintessential dream maker because he challenged all of our expectations and helped us grow up to be great young men. Not just on the football field, but in all of life. He taught us the most important elements to leading a successful life: the "hows."

How to dream and chase those dreams.
How to develop a path to success.
How to follow that plan step-by-step.
How to grow both personally and as a team.

After I graduated from high school, as my grandfather continued to fight ALS, I joined a summer baseball league. At eighteen, I definitely didn't have the world by the tail. It had me. I was lost and directionless. Then, one night following one of our games, a gruff, burly man approached me. He had a cigar on one side of his mouth, a plug of tobacco in the opposite cheek, and a dip crammed behind his front lip. I am pretty certain the surgeon general had a poster of him in his Washington office as the embodiment of unhealthy habits to rail against.

He was the late Jack Allen, head baseball coach at Ranger Junior College in Ranger, Texas. Coach Allen offered me a chance to chase my dream after I had seemingly run out of them.

"I'm going to give you a scholarship," he said. "I know you want to be a ballplayer. I know about your grandparents, I know about your grades. You come play for me."

There was a sign outside of Ranger Junior College for a long time that said, "Ranger. Reading, writing, and Rodeo." That's where I went to school.

Coach Allen's deal was that he was going to put me on the team and get me into classes that I could pass. In return, I would play baseball for him during the week with the option of going home on the weekends to spend time with my grandparents. So, in the summer of 1982, that's what I did for the next four-and-a-half months.

Every weekend that first semester, I went home to be with my grandfather, Ernest Morris. With each passing week his strong frame withered away just a little more. When someone so big and powerful, someone who is such an overwhelming presence in your life, is reduced to utter dependence and is diminished just a little with each passing breath, it makes an impression on you—a lasting one.

On the last Sunday of November, I kissed my grandparents goodbye at midnight, and headed back to Ranger Junior College so that I could make my 8 a.m. class in the morning. I got back to the school at about 1 a.m.

Then at about 3 a.m., Coach Allen jostled me awake.

"You need to go home," he said. "Ernest has passed away. You go home and take care of your grandmother, take care of the funeral. Your grandmother has done enough."

In the fall of 1982, Ernest Morris left this earth. People came from all over the country to pay tribute to a man they knew who lived for other people. After he was buried, I never returned to Ranger or to the baseball team.

❧

From the time I was a young child, I was told I was stupid. And I believed it. My dad told me I was an idiot, usually with a four-letter word attached, my whole life. My guidance counselor told me I was too dumb to get into college. Yet aside from talent, or a lack thereof, there was a reason for this alleged intellectual inadequacy.

With our countless relocations from town to town and city to city due to my dad's inability to hold down a naval assignment, I was constantly switching schools. I would learn a concept in one place only to relocate to a different school where they'd be on a different concept. I was always lost, always playing catch-up.

That was before I studied under Dr. Roth (anatomy), and Dr. Byrd (physiology) at Howard Payne University—two dream makers who helped me discover talents I never knew I had. When I entered college, I immediately enrolled in anatomy and physiology, two of the most challenging courses offered. Dr. Roth was a doctor in our community, and he taught a class of twenty students. Nineteen of them were registered nurses. Then there was me.

After our first test, Dr. Roth asked me to stay after class.

"You need to go to medical school," he said after handing me my test.

"I'm not smart enough," I said.

"I just graded your test and your answers were better and more thoughtful than the questions I wrote," Dr. Roth replied. "In this room, there are nineteen nurses and they all want to be your lab partner. What does that say?"

"It says I look good."

"You can be anything you want to be."

Dr. Byrd said much the same. Those were the first two teachers I ever had that led me to figure out that, you know what? I'm not dumb. I finally had someone in the academic realm who believed in me. That's when school became fun. I didn't feel like I was at a disadvantage. I took that anatomy class over the summer. Nobody wanted to ruin their summer by taking anatomy because it was such a difficult class. I aced it.

Roberto Hernandez from the Devil Rays was another dream maker. A big right-handed pitcher at 6'4", Hernandez had arms down to his knees. When he released the ball, it looked like his hand was right on top of the plate. On our roster, I was a set-up guy; he was a closer. I just remember watching him warm up with his power and accuracy and thinking to myself, "Good Lord. What did I just see?"

We hung out together. We'd go eat together. He mentored me, giving me advice on what to expect and what not to expect. When we were in Seattle, he told me not to use the shampoo in the locker room or the iron in my hotel room.

Good advice. I discovered that some players had a habit of pissing in the irons in the hotel and doing the same in the shampoo bottles in the locker room. So I took my own shampoo with me from then on, and wore shirts that were less than crisp. Bert always shared little tips like that, pointers that could make the difference between a good day and a day from hell.

Then there was first baseman Fred McGriff, and shortstop Ozzie Guillen. I used game film of these guys to show my high school players how to and how not to do things. Nevertheless, they each took me in as one of their own.

This hit me profoundly right from the start during my debut game against the Texas Rangers at the Ballpark at Arlington—where I was living my dream in front of everyone I knew and loved. After the game I walked into the clubhouse. Devil Rays third baseman and Hall of Famer Wade Boggs was there. He hugged me and said, "Man, that is just the greatest baseball story we've ever heard."

"But you're Wade Boggs," I replied, starstruck and dumbfounded.

When we faced the Mariners in Seattle, the guys would bring their golf clubs and their fly-fishing poles. On our days off we'd golf and fish. In truth, we were just a bunch of boys who got paid a crap load of money to play a kid's game.

But it wasn't all fun and games. There was a lot of pressure. Players were always looking over their shoulder at the new crop coming up, guys who could easily knock them off the roster if they let their level of play slip. This was especially true for players who had been playing consistently for a decade or more, who hadn't taken a break from the pressure to live life.

For me, the experience in the big leagues was just icing on the cake. For a short period of time I got to play a game I'd wanted to play since I was a little boy—on the big stage.

I had a book written and a movie made about me—all because I took the less traveled back roads into the majors. There was never any pressure on me, I wasn't supposed to be there anyway. Through their grace under professional stress, those guys helped me realize that the actualization of my boyhood aspiration was far more special than the dream ever was. They also became dream makers.

◦◦◦

A few months after I moved in to my grandparent's house in Brownwood, Texas, we loaded a stack of presents into their car. It was Christmas Eve and we drove together to a house in town, the home of a family who had been strapped financially. We stopped at the curb and my grandparents unloaded the presents, stacking them neatly on the porch.

As soon as they were finished arranging the packages, they rang the doorbell and scrambled towards the car, jumping into the backseat at the last second. As the designated getaway driver, I stomped on the gas and sped away. It was awesome watching my grandparents run like a couple of teenage pranksters!

That's who my grandparents, Ernest and Alice Morris, were. They would cook thanksgiving dinners for families who couldn't afford holiday meals, and pay utility bills for people who had trouble making their monthly nut. They did this anonymously. These families never knew where the money or the meals came from.

My grandparents didn't want any credit. They did it because they could, and they wanted to. They both grew up in houses with dirt floors, no indoor plumbing, and no electricity. Though they weren't rich, they had reached a point in their lives where they could give back. It filled them with a sense of gratitude that they wanted to share.

Early on, I didn't know these things about my grandparents. After my father was transferred from Hollywood, Florida, to Brownwood to work as a navy recruiter, my parents stayed back in Florida for a short time. I was sent on ahead to live with my grandparents so that I could begin working with the football team under Coach Wood and prepare for high school.

I later learned that my mother was the driving force behind the transfer. McArthur High School, where I went to school in Hollywood, was pretty rough. I was targeted by certain ethic groups and my mother feared I would get hurt or fall in with a bad crowd.

At first, I dreaded the move. *Oh my God, these are my father's parents*, I thought to myself. *He turned out the way he did for a reason. They're going to be the same way he is.*

Nothing could have been further from the truth. I went from watching two people argue, curse, throw things, and hit each other, to watching a couple cherish and build each other up in integrity, trust, and love. Over the course of the three years I lived with them, I never heard my grandparents say a harsh word to each other. They never uttered anything they couldn't take back. Now, they were old school, so there were days of silence.

When I arrived at my grandparents' house, I went from taking care of the yard, making sure the house was in order, overseeing my little brother, and living under an arbitrary set of rules, to having a few routine chores and just two directives: 1) if you do it, own it, get it over with, and move on; and 2) if you always tell the truth, you won't have to remember what you said because the truth is the truth.

I never knew what would set my parents off. At my grandparent's house, if I followed their two rules, all was good. My grandfather was 6'3" and weighed in at 260 pounds. He fought in World War II, and saw things no one would ever want to see. After coming home from the war, he bought a home in Brownwood and started a family.

That house was a small, post-World War II cookie cutter home with an attached carport. It was on a single level with a living room, kitchen, and office on one side, and a master bedroom, bathroom, and two small bedrooms on the other. It smelled faintly of propane on account of the gas space heaters stationed in various rooms. Window unit air conditioners kept it cool in the sweltering summer—no central heating or air. It was the first house in my life that I ever felt safe. For me, the shift in atmosphere was disorienting.

My grandparents were both fantastic cooks. On the weekdays, my grandmother prepared the meals, while on weekends my grandfather grilled steaks and tossed together a delicious pea salad, a recipe I prepare to this day.

Though he was big and tall, I never heard my grandfather raise his voice. But he commanded attention. His charisma, magnetism, and caring heart were so irresistible, people wanted to pay attention to him.

My grandmother, at 5'3", was not as imposing. But she was just as powerful. The secretary for Central United Methodist Church for more than thirty years, she was one of the smartest people I have ever known. She could do trigonometry in her head, a capability that apparently skipped a couple of generations. I did not receive that gift.

My grandparents had a powerful effect on people, seemingly always drawing out the best in them. People strived not to disappoint them. In fact, my father was nicer to me in the presence of my grandfather. He was even more pleasant to me when my grandmother was around.

My grandfather made me take my grandmother out on lunch dates once per week over the three years I attended Brownwood High School. He wanted to make sure I knew how to treat women. I learned how to open car doors and restaurant doors for her, pull out chairs, unfold napkins, and stand when she approached and left the table. I learned how to keep her on the inside of the sidewalk and away from traffic as we walked down the street.

My grandfather taught me these things, and then he graded me on my performance. But that's not the worst part; my grandmother graded me first. I didn't even like school, and now I was being graded outside of school. Twice.

My grandfather launched his menswear store from the ground up on a handshake.

"If this was anybody else asking for a loan, I would not approve it," the banker told him. "But I know you will pay me back." And he did. Every penny.

For three summers, I worked at my grandfather's store, learning something new almost every day. Back in the day when there were just three television channels and we were the remote control, there was this guy on TV known as "The Singing Cowboy." One day, that man walked into my grandfather's store. I recognized him right away. He walked up to my grandfather and hugged him like they were best friends. That man was Gene Autry. He and my grandfather had fought in the war together. Dallas Cowboys head coach Tom Landry bought hats from my grandfather and wore them on the sidelines during Cowboys games.

One morning, a lady walked into my grandfather's store at 9:05 a.m. She was dressed in a cowboy hat, overalls, and a pair of muddy boots. Judging by the smell wafting from those boots, she had a pig farm. All of the men who worked for my grandfather were seated in the back of the store. They looked up from their coffee, got a look at this woman, and immediately went back to sipping from their steaming cups. It was like she didn't exist.

My grandfather saw this from his office, got up, and walked out to meet her. He asked what she was looking for and showed her a few selected suits that were hanging on the racks. Before she left his store, she had purchased fifteen suits, one for every male member of her family. She paid in cash.

"Don't ever, ever judge anyone by their appearance," my grandfather said as he walked by me after the sale. "It doesn't matter if they dig ditches, or they're the president. Treat everyone like you would treat your grandmother."

That woman came into my grandfather's store every year after that to buy suits for her family, all because of how she was treated by my grandfather that fateful day. A few years later, prospectors discovered natural gas underneath her pig farm, a find worth $800 million.

My grandfather taught me that the most important person at any given moment is the person standing right in front of you. They deserve 100 percent of your attention.

He also stressed that if I ever made a promise, I must live up to that promise—no matter what. Because at the end of your life when you pass away, you'll be remembered for the answer to one question: did you live by your word, and were you honest? It takes a lifetime to build character, and one mistake can destroy everything you've ever worked for.

Today, we're so busy staring at our smartphones reading texts and social media posts that we forget that people—with their eye movements and facial expressions—are real. My grandfather's smartphone was a Rolodex. He recorded every customer's name and measurements on that Rolodex.

Thirty-five years after my grandfather's store had closed, I was giving a speech in Houston speaking about my grandfather, and how so few people behaved that way anymore. Nobody gave back. Everybody just wanted to leverage the moment to his or her advantage. After I finished my speech, a ninety-five-year-old man approached me. He had tears in his eyes.

"I knew your grandfather," he said. And he opened up his jacket to show me the label on his inside breast pocket. Ernest Morris Menswear, it read.

At fifteen, I was angry and resentful. I could have easily gone off the rails. "Not today," my grandfather stressed. "What are you going to do when you can't throw a baseball hard anymore?"

"Well, I'll play quarterback," I said.

"What are you going to do when you can't throw the ball to people anymore?"

At eighteen you think that will never happen. Then sometime around the age of forty, you have to get up and pee four times a night and you realize you can't throw a ball hard anymore or connect with receivers.

Around that same time during my senior year in high school, I got some bad news. My grandfather was diagnosed with ALS, and it all started with just a stumble in his store. He went from striding confidently, to walking with the support of a cane, to being confined to a wheelchair, all within the span of just six months. I watched him go from confidently leading the people in his community while being a member of virtually every board in the county, to struggling to lead people from his wheelchair. He never once complained about the disease that was quickly draining the life out of him.

Before the illness took his voice, my grandfather and I were sitting in his kitchen one evening. He was stooped over in his wheelchair, struggling to take breaths from a tube hooked up to an oxygen bottle.

"How could this happen to such a good man?" I asked with resentful intensity. "You've done nothing but help people your entire life. You've pulled people from holes and they have no idea who it was that pulled them out. Why did God do this to you?"

My grandfather took in some oxygen and looked up at me as best he could.

"I've worked my whole life to get to where I'm going," he said. "Where are you headed?"

The last time he attended Central United Methodist Church, I carried him into the nave. He couldn't move, but he sure could smile. If it weren't for all of the people in Brownwood who committed to help take care of him as he declined, I don't know if my grandmother could have coped.

After he died in November of 1982, people came from all over the country to pay their respects to a man they knew lived for other people. If we all had sentiments like that carved on our tombstones, how great a country would this be?

∽∾

While I was in the midst of living my dream, my wife Lorri and I both knew the chasm between us was insurmountable. We were still married on paper and our children needed us, just not together. We were a couple, completely different, with zero in common except for our kids.

In the movie *The Rookie*, we were portrayed as the all-American family who had achieved the all-American success story: love, close family, and a dream that came true. But that narrative was far from the truth. Fortunately, the book, the movie, and my experiences on the fringes of that surreal world known as Hollywood kept me pleasantly distracted from that reality. I was consumed with consulting on the film, and with publicity tours. But underneath my stoic veneer, I suffered from pervasive loneliness and probably grief.

That's when the next dream maker entered my life. My stepsister Laura Harris, daughter of my mother's second husband, must have realized how I was suffering, because she constantly talked-up her co-worker Shawna Gray. They both worked at Ferguson Enterprises, a nationwide bathroom and kitchen plumbing and appliance dealer. Laura was in outside sales while Shawna worked inside sales at the company's Dallas Design District showroom.

At the time, Laura and her husband Gary had been married twenty-four years. They were soul mates. They met in high school and married young, had four children, and are together to this day. They beat the odds. Their love story seems to have inspired Laura's belief that true love was possible for everyone. Even me.

I wasn't as optimistic. Plus, I was conflicted. Though I was lonely, my responsibility to my children and the failure of my marriage gnawed at me. I despised failure. On a surface level, it wasn't all that difficult. But underneath, I was miserable. Plus, my budding fame from the book and movie allowed me a much-needed distraction. At the same time, I felt strongly that a new relationship would unnecessarily complicate my life.

I tried dating an old flame and instantly discovered the pitfalls of celebrity. Some women turn into giggling groupies around famous people. Of course, I realized the fleetingness of my fame and its importance—or lack thereof. It wasn't like I had cured cancer or discovered something that would change the course of humanity. I was just an aging athlete who had the ability to throw a baseball with blinding speed. It seemed odd to me that women fawned all over me and I grew to abhor the falseness of it. It also played on my own insecurities. Did people want to be friends with me, or the Rookie?

As strange as it sounds, I found myself feeling sorry for Hollywood stars. How could they possibly recognize true friends? One time at an event in Las Vegas for Russell

Athletics—one of the movie's sponsors—Dennis Quaid and I were crammed in a room for 200 people with what felt like 1,000. They were all over us.

"Want to get out of here?' Dennis asked.

"Yes!" I answered. We could hardly move. We had to fight our way out of the room, all the while being grabbed for pictures with the attendees. Some were nice. Others were not. I was out of my element.

We walked down to the casino and Dennis began playing blackjack at an empty table. Before I could blink there were hundreds of people surrounding that table. I realized then that I was with a mega-star. How do they do this every day? I had no use for any of it.

Shawna and I finally met on a blind date in August of 2000. My stepsister had asked her if she was free one weekend that month. She urged Shawna and I to join her and her husband on a double date.

Shawna knew I was a celebrity of sorts. Though she didn't pay attention to sports and had no clue about my story, she'd seen me on the cover of *Guidepost* magazine and had heard Laura's stories about me. In that picture, I was tossing a ball up in the air and she saw my wedding ring on the finger of my throwing hand. She couldn't get that ring out of her mind. Shawna was divorced with two children: Zach, age eleven, and Chelsey, age five. She was a single mom just trying to survive. She didn't need me and that ring complicating her life further.

Though she was hesitant, she finally accepted Laura's offer. She knew I was a man of faith, so we shared that in common, which put her at ease somewhat. The three of us arrived at her house in my pickup truck. She thought I was mysterious, the strong, silent type but extremely polite and charming—the quintessential Texan. She didn't even mind my constant tobacco chewing, a habit I took up a notch when I was nervous. Which I was.

We started things off at Uncle Julio's "Mexican food from scratch." I ordered a Dos Equis Lager Especial in the green bottle.

"Why did you order the green one? Why not the brown?" she asked.

"Because the brown one tastes like shit," I snarked. I guess she was amused by my candor.

After we chatted it up for a while, I gently leaned toward her.

"You smell nice," I whispered. She blushed.

We continued our evening in Dallas' West End district at a karaoke bar before we ended up at a country western dance hall where we two-stepped all over the floor. Two women ogled me as we went through our moves, no doubt recognizing my "Rookie" persona. I could tell it made Shawna uncomfortable, maybe even a bit jealous. She liked me.

Over the next couple of weeks, I turned on the charm, sending her flowers and taking her out for lunch. During the baseball off-season, I drove up to Dallas from San Angelo every weekend to see her. One day she gave me a tour of the Ferguson showroom, and explained that she could help me build my dream home.

"Well it would be yours too, so sure," I said.

She balked at the idea, no doubt thinking I was moving too fast. But I knew already that I loved her and wanted her to be my wife. There was something in her, something I had never experienced before.

Then several months later, without notice, I fell off the face of the earth. No visits. No calls, notes, or flowers. I know this confused and frustrated her. But I was going through a slow-motion train-wreck of a break-up with Lorri, had three little kids to take care of, and was consumed with the production of *The Rookie*.

It was supposed to be the best time of my life, but it was simultaneously the worst. To this add my anguish over doing exactly what my parents had done: split. I couldn't deal with all of that. I couldn't put it into words. I wanted to be like my grandparents and have a successful, long-lasting union. I had just chosen the wrong person.

After two years of stalling and dodging—and perhaps, not ironically, after the book and movie were released—Lorri and I were finally divorced. Shawna and I were married in November of 2002. It was a small affair with family and a few close friends at Preston Road Church of Christ in Dallas, just a few blocks from Southern Methodist University. Our five kids, ages thirteen to four, were flower girls and ring bearers. One of the best parts of the ceremony was when we, as a new family, held hands and committed ourselves to each other. The other best part was walking down the aisle as husband and wife. We had made it through some difficult times while dating and we had no idea what lay ahead.

When I think of our marital vows, I joke to Shawna that she took me in sickness and in sickness. There hasn't been much health for her to take. In our nearly two decades of marriage, I've gone through more than thirty different doctors, had more than fifty surgeries, and endured an endless series of tests.

At various times, I've been in excruciating physical pain, had migraines that lasted months on end, had no sense of taste or smell, have lost my ability to speak, and been constrained by a limited ability to move (as a professional athlete this was one of the worst symptoms). I've been prescribed and taken an endless quantity of narcotics and other medications. Not one of those doctors seemed to know what was wrong with me.

Through all of these insufferable trials, Shawna stood by me as we tried to find some reason for all my suffering. She took me to—and stood by me for—countless doctor's appointments, procedures, and surgeries. She nursed be back to health so that I could face the next challenge. She's been my biggest advocate. As I've flown to destinations for speaking engagements from coast to coast and country to country, she's been with me each and every time. She's heard me tell the same stories over and over, and helped me craft new ones. Each time she's accompanied me with genuine enthusiasm and support. She's also my manager. When I tell people that I get to sleep with my manager, she cringes, elbows me, and giggles. We are a great team.

After enduring all of that, she's still by my side. Not because I'm a famous athlete or a guy who's had a movie made about him, but because she loves me for me. She's the one who didn't give up.

I've experienced the best and worst of times simultaneously: the best because of her, and the worst because of my health. On the day I was finally diagnosed with Parkinson's, we looked at each other and wept. But along with those tears was a sense of relief because we finally understood what we were up against. Without her, I could not have carried out this fight. Without her, I would have never made it to The Treatment Center.

Multiple times over the years—two within the span of this writing—I've come within an inch of death. Time and time again Shawna and my faith have helped me overcome these dark times. I know this, that God has a plan for me, because if he did not, Shawna would not be in my life, I wouldn't be sharing my story all over the world, and I wouldn't be here. After all I have been through, there's no earthly reason why I should be alive right now.

In baseball, the team wins the game. In marriage, we face and overcome our challenges together. And so far, we are winning. Shawna is the hero in my story.

⌘

Dream makers are those people who want to see you succeed if for no other reason than the thrill they get watching someone go further than they thought was possible. They want to see you achieve and share the moment your dream becomes a reality. They want to see your eyes light up and hear you holler with joy as you drink in your achievement.

Dream makers are the people you want in your corner invoking the most daring prayers on your behalf. Surround yourself with these people so you can be the best version of yourself possible. At the same time, dream makers know the power of remaining humble and the importance of remembering who you are. Dream makers are God's gift to us in this life, and tangible confirmation of His presence.

CHAPTER 7

MENTORING THE DREAM

If we're giving of our talents—making somebody else better—we're a mentor. If we function as a mentor, we're a dream maker. And if we're a dream maker, we're going to watch people go out into the world and do things they didn't think they could do.

In 1997, I found myself at Reagan County High School in Big Lake, Texas after my wife Lorri came home with a job listing for an assistant football and head baseball coach at the school. Big Lake is about seventy-one miles west of San Angelo. The two towns are strung together by Highway 67, a barren strip bordered by scrub and hundreds of deer that often become heaps of road kill.

Big Lake is an oil and gas town, its surroundings burnt, dusty, and flat. You could add sterile, too, save for the poles strung with power cables and telephone lines and the water tower emblazoned with Reagan County High's owl mascot. Most of the businesses in Big Lake had their fortunes tied to oil and gas exploration and production, supplying things like derricks, pig valves, milling tools, and welding services. There was also an office supply store, a Dairy Queen, City Hall, a fire station, and the Reagan County brick court-house, erected in 1927.

Big Lake was a town infested with clouds of sandy dust stirred up by howling winds bouncing off the *caliche*, a natural sedimentary cement composed of gravel, sand, clay, and silt. That grit stuck to everything. It got on your clothes, in your car, and in your house. It even got inside of me. Every time I blew my nose I blasted out a stream of mud—an inspiring memory.

Big Lake had a population of roughly 2,858 at that time, down sharply from its peak of 3,699 in 1990, though it recovered to 3,239 by 2017. The latter figure is no doubt due to the recent West Texas oil boom. That population is made up mostly of oil and gas workers and ranchers. Teachers, coaches, and government workers round out the rest of Big Lake's inhabitants, along with those employed by the car dealership and the Mustang Motel.

Ironically enough, Dennis Quaid and Meg Ryan, then husband and wife, had holed up in the Mustang for several weeks during the filming of *Flesh and Bone*, a gritty 1993 neo noir film set in rural Texas. Big Lake was one of the film's shooting locations and the locals continued to talk about their fifteen minutes of fame when I got there.

The thing I remember most about Big Lake was the smell. The place had this persistent aroma of chemical fumes that gave me a pounding headache the first two months I lived there. Aspirin, Tylenol, nothing could touch it.

"I can't get rid of this headache," I said to David Steele, the high school's athletic director and head football coach. "It's been killing me ever since I got here."

"Don't worry," he said. "It'll go way in another week or so." Steele explained that the headaches were from the vapors discharged from a nearby gas plant. "You get used to it and the headaches go away."

They did.

We moved into a Spartan three-bedroom house. When I say "we," I mean my son Hunter and me. Lorri stayed back in San Angelo with Jessica so she wouldn't have a 140-mile round trip commute to her job at Angelo State every day. At night, the horizon was candle-lit with flames from oil well gas burn off. The fields where those flames burned were worked mostly by Latino immigrants, and their kids filled the classrooms at Reagan County High.

The strangest thing about Big Lake is its name. There's really no body of water there to speak of, and certainly not one you could consider big. The town was named after a dry lake two miles south, situated atop the divide between the Rio Grande and Colorado River watersheds. That waterless lake is the largest of its kind in Texas.

There was an actual lake there in the 1930s, 1950s, and again in the 1970s, filled mostly from high-runoff rain events. But it baked off in the intervening years, leaving a 1,000-acre dusty basin since about 1977. A few years before I got there to work at the school, some prankster posted a sign in the lakebed: "Who pulled the plug on Big Lake?"

As those population figures attest, the town was in the midst of a downturn when I arrived. J.R. Dunn, Big Lake's mayor at the time, proposed refilling the lake by drilling scores of wells to bring water to the surface from 650 feet below the lakebed. The goal was to stoke a tourism boom. But the plan went bust before the first hole was drilled. The costs were prohibitive. I wondered why anyone would ever live in the Godforsaken place when I'd passed through on my way to Arizona more than a decade before. I still didn't know.

Some of the teachers at the high school asked me that same question.

"Why did you take this job? Nobody wants to work here," they said.

"Well, why are *you* working here?" I shot back.

"Because we get paid more than anybody else in the state for living out here."

Wow, I thought to myself. *You're not even in it for the kids.*

Reagan County High School had an impressive football stadium, green and well-maintained. The baseball field was another matter. It was little more than a scrub-infested sandlot—emblematic of West Texas priorities. The fences were in disrepair. The outfield was teeming with goat heads, a small bush weed with sharp pointy burs. The infield was a little more than a solid crust of caliche. Both the infield and outfield were on uneven ground. This was no field of dreams.

In addition to my coaching duties, I would teach integrated physics and chemistry at Reagan County High School. The school was run down, a single level utilitarian structure with two hallways. In truth, I thought Big Lake was a freakin' dive. But that windswept piece of desolation humbled me. It reordered my priorities and put me on a path that was both profoundly transformational and rewarding.

One of the first things I noticed about Big Lake was that the town's slumping fortunes were reflected in the outlook of my players. Those kids never expected to ever get out of high school. They had no hope. No, it was worse than that. They didn't know how to hope, or what it even meant to hope.

"Coach, we're going to work in the oil and gas fields like our dads and granddads did and there's nothing you or anyone else can do about it," one of them said to me. "We're stuck. People come through here on their way to somewhere else."

For most of their lives these kids had been snubbed and talked down to by the coaching staff, their teachers, and sometimes their parents. That first season, I had eight of those kids show up for the baseball team. I don't know how much you may know about baseball, but eight is not enough.

"Coach, we only won one game each year for the three years before you got here," another one of them said. "We're in trouble. They are going to cut the money for our program to give more to football."

We were in desperate shape. So I begged and borrowed to get two more kids to bring our team up to ten players to get through the season. They could not throw. They could not hit. They could barely run. I got two more players after they became eligible under the Texas "No Pass/No Play" rules by improving their grades.

Now I had a team.

But their grumbling frustrated me. And my job was made harder after the school board met and voted to purge the coaching staff in the wake of a winless football season.

Coach David Steele was out. I was spared because I was hired primarily to coach the baseball team.

Steele's replacement as athletic director and head football coach was Scott Simpson, a former college football player who had coached for some fifteen years. His most recent coaching stint up to that time was as an assistant at Mesquite High School, just east of Dallas.

Simpson was big—six foot three and just a few pounds south of 300. He had never been a head coach before, and now he was athletic director to boot. He burned with determination and was eager to prove himself. He reminded me a lot of Brownwood's Gordon Wood. They were both excellent coaches. Both believed in bellowing at players to get results. And both believed baseball was blight upon the hallowed Texas ground.

It may come as a shock, but coach Simpson and I did not see eye to eye.

Yet despite that emerging friction, I was still determined to knock the defeatist attitude out of my team. I knew I had to if we were going to make it as a cohesive unit. I had to light a fire in their sorry bellies, inspire them to go beyond what they thought they could do and be. But how?

I had two things going for me: my status as a former professional player in the minor leagues and my popularity in the classroom. To that, add my mild-mannered coaching style on the field. These things gave me credibility. At first, these kids were skeptical. They thought I was like everybody else: out to diss and badger them.

But I listened to them and told them they were good. They knew I was there for them and I wasn't in it for the money, or because Big Lake was a breathtakingly beautiful destination. I treated them with respect. When they addressed me, I responded with "yes sir" and "no ma'am." They were shocked.

They always knew where I stood. There were no hidden agendas. They trusted me. Eventually, they would come to me with their hidden problems and concerns, issues they would never dare bring to anyone else.

Now I had to figure out how to turn that trust around and get them to believe in themselves. The first thing these kids needed was a little self-regard. "If you don't respect yourselves, no one else is going to respect you," I said to them. They had to learn that they were not the enemy. Neither was I.

I taught them how to wear their uniforms properly. I insisted they pull up their pants to where they belonged, take off their jewelry, and turn their caps around so that the bills were facing the front.

"When you get a multi-million-dollar contract on a Major League team," I told them, "that's when you can flaunt your bling and turn your cap. But until then we're going to look good and build each other up. We're going to act like a team. One team."

Once we had the basics of self-respect down, I told them about the importance of respecting others, namely their teachers. That meant opening doors for them, responding with "yes ma'am" and "no sir," turning their homework in on time, and otherwise keeping their mouths closed. They were in school to learn, and they had to take advantage of every opportunity that learning presented if they were going to succeed on the field and at life beyond Big Lake.

After that lesson, I charged them with taking care of our field. "This is our home," I said. "This is where other teams come to try and beat us." If we aren't proud of our home turf, if we don't have a stake in its viability as a field of play, how could we credibly defend it?

So we got to work. I tapped the knowhow of baseball coaches, ground crewmen and horticulturalists, and bought tools and seed. I enlisted the players, their parents, and a few volunteers from town to tend the grounds. The infield and outfield grasses were infested with weeds and gravel. It was dangerous to run on and you wouldn't dare slide into a base on this treacherous surface. So we got down on our hands and knees to pull weeds and clear rocks. We dug out three inches of caliche from the infield surface and I bought fresh dirt and had it trucked in from Oklahoma to replace it.

We planted annual grasses on the field. We didn't have an aerator, so I had my players put on spikes and run back and forth across the field to make holes in the ground so that the seed would take. When I came to school early one morning to water the seed, I spotted there were deer all over the field when I turned on the lights. They were feeding on the grass seed.

That's when a group of guys from the local barbershop decided to pitch in. They gathered up all of the human hair clippings, stuffed them into plastic bags, and we spread the hair all over so that the human scent would repel the deer. It worked.

Appearances are important. I believed that if we built it, they would come—players, parents, and towns folk. If we built it, they would win. By the first day of practice, the grass was as green as that grass growing on the prized football field.

We worked on pitching and batting, and ran fielding drills so that they could learn how to properly cover the bases. To get their swings in synch with pitches, we worked relentlessly on batting practice. I figured the best way to judge their swings and offer corrective measures was from the pitcher's mound. So I did the pitching.

"Coach, you're too fast," they moaned. "Are you trying to kill us?"

I laughed at their grumbling, thinking I wasn't throwing any faster or harder than the average high school pitcher. I wound up and threw even harder the more they complained. Then I'd toss a slow curve to keep them on their toes.

They needed practice and I strived to make our practices fun. They were like parties with purpose, and we kept our focus on excellence.

When my players were working practice drills, I was on the field with them working those same drills. If they didn't get what I was teaching, I showed them how to do it. It's not just talking the talk; it's walking the walk.

I didn't bellow at them. Football, basketball, and track coaches had been shrieking at these kids so often and for so long that they were immune to loud voices. Their howls went in one ear and out the other. My style was quiet. I sensed that they would listen to instructions if they weren't dispatched angrily and at high volume.

I told them they were good, even though they weren't. But they didn't need to hear what they were. They needed to hear what they could be. I told them they had it in them to win, to exceed expectations—which I made sure were high. They needed inspiration and motivation. Everybody does.

This was in stark contrast to the previous baseball coach. His training, my players told me, mostly involved the batting machine. He had them set it to 90 miles per hour and he taught them how to encroach on the ball so that they would be awarded first base on a "hit by pitch." He had so little faith in their latent abilities—was so indifferent to the potential for injury—that he didn't even try to teach them how to develop the necessary skills to win. He cheated them.

We marshaled our ragtag skills, inspiration, and motivation to mount a winning start to the season. After entering a tournament in Sonora, a hundred miles southeast of Big Lake, we made the finals, only to be knocked out of the series by a score of 6 to 5 against an excellent team. On the bus ride home the team was buzzed, whooping and hollering. We'd now played ten games, losing only three.

"Hey coach, we really are pretty good," one of them said. But things crumbled as the season unfurled. Still, after having won just one game in each of the previous three seasons, we concluded my inaugural season as coach with a win-loss record of ten and fourteen. At home, we were ten and zero. Nobody beat us on our home turf. This really was our field of dreams.

But as my first season as coach of the Owls was getting into full swing, my relationship with Lorri was running aground on matrimonial shoals. She was pregnant and that just added to the stress and interpersonal friction. The cracks and sharp rocks that littered the space between us seemed to multiply with her expanding belly. The silences, those moments—sometimes long—when we were in the same room without saying a word to each other, were deafening. So, we avoided them by working late and running errands.

We made perfunctory attempts to salvage what was left. I asked Lorri to come watch my baseball team play a game, promising I'd have her home before dark. I wanted her to see me succeed at something. We won the game and when we got home, she complained her leg was wet. She was only six months pregnant. What if her water had broken? She looked worried after she came out of the bathroom.

"I think I'd better go to the hospital," she said. After she was checked out, medical staff determined that the liquid was not amniotic fluid. She was sent home. When she awoke in the middle of the night, the bed was soaking wet. We had to get her back to the hospital. We called her mother to stay with the kids and rushed to San Angelo Community Medical Center. Now tests showed that the discharge was definitely amniotic fluid. But San Angelo Community didn't have neonatal facilities.

So she had to be transported to Harris Methodist Hospital in Fort Worth by air ambulance—a small twin-engine turboprop. Lorri was sedated for the flight. The paramedics crouched beside her. I squeezed into tiny area in the back of the airplane, a space reserved for small cargo. I wedged myself in. There was no seatbelt back there. None was needed.

It was a wild ride. On approach to Meacham International Airport just north of downtown Fort Worth, the aircraft abruptly banked sideways. Maybe it was due to a vortex generated by the wake of a plane that had just landed.

I don't know. But I fully expected the downward wing to scrape the ground and catapult us into a violent catastrophe.

So did the paramedics. I could read the same terror on their faces that I felt rippling in my cramped gut. I'm not sure my life was flashing before my eyes, but the pre-feature trailers were sure rolling. The pilot somehow recovered control of the aircraft and we touched down without incident. It was a harrowing start to this rollercoaster birth drama. When you think about it, it's amazing I continue to walk jetways sixty to seventy times per year boarding flights to my speaking gigs.

When we arrived at Harris Methodist, the staff obstetrician said the baby—a girl—was too small to deliver. So they administered special drugs and told Lorri she would have to remain flat on her back for several weeks. I opted to stay in Fort Worth while my team was in the thick of the baseball season. My assistant Bo Comacho, a hard driving Latino who played college football as a linebacker, was managing the team. My players didn't take to his style. Their play suffered and they lost most of the remaining games that season. I felt bad for my team and how their high hopes at the beginning of the season crashed and burned by the end.

My mother drove my car up to Fort Worth so that I could drive back and retrieve test papers, lesson plans, and my grade book. She also brought Hunter and Jessica for a few visits.

Jaimee was born six weeks premature. She weighed in at only three pounds, nine ounces and spent the first week of her life in an incubator. She had blond hair and blue eyes and was so small; she disappeared behind my gloved hand.

It was agonizing to watch this tiny precious baby struggle to hang on to the tenuous thread of life she was gifted. I tried to be as supportive a husband, teacher, coach, and father as I possibly could while I grappled with the crisis.

But I won't pretend it was easy, or that at times it didn't take more out of me than I thought I could give. Lorri and I hadn't been on the same wavelength for a long time, if we ever had been. And Jaimee seemed to embody that rift and our struggle to cope with it. That's a terrible burden for a child to suffer, even if the both of us unknowingly, or, subconsciously, inflicted this upon her.

But through our struggles, rocky parental challenges, and many prayers, Jaimee and I grew extremely close over the ensuing years. As of this writing, we are planning her wedding, and her mother and I couldn't be more proud of her and her life choices.

෴

At the start of my second season as coach, sixty-three kids tried out for the baseball team, a number that included scorekeepers and those running the scoreboard. I had more kids come out for my team than Scott Simpson did for his football team. This did not make him happy.

Hunter and I decamped from our Big Lake house and moved back to San Angelo to be with the rest of the family. Now I endured a 140-mile commute.

Before that pivotal second season started, we launched the next phase of our field refurbishment. We tended the infield with tweezers and scissors, repaired the netting on the batting cages, and painted the dugouts and team benches. We also mended and replaced the fencing around those dugouts. In the outfield, we rebuilt and covered the centerfield fence with a coat of blue, emblazoning it with our mascot—the Owls.

It isn't easy to create a mean-looking owl, but our school nurse, Mary Joe Cockrell, who was also an artist, was up to the task. That owl looked vicious. I liked to think it intimidated visiting teams. The resurrection of the baseball field became the talk of Big Lake. People pulled into the parking lot just to see for themselves.

But that surge of pride was short-lived.

While on my way to practice one day just before the baseball season had officially begun, Scott Simpson pulled me aside. "You've taken these kids as far as you can," he said. "They're losers. Their parents are losers. They're never going to amount to anything."

Then he punched his finger into my chest. "If they're ever close to winning or behind, these kids will find a way to fail. You may be a great baseball coach, but you're always going to come in last behind people like me because you're too nice. And nice people finish last. They'll never do what you tell them to do. You'll see."

I seethed. This betrayal and smear of my players came from the school's athletic director. What's worse, two of my players who were on their way to practice overheard what Simpson said. Before I could get to the field and attempt damage control, the message had spread through team like wildfire. Coach Simpson destroyed eighteen months of hard work in two minutes. I was right back at square one, except now I had sixty-three of these kids instead of just a dozen.

With this incident, I had reached the point where just the sight of Simpson filled me with rage.

During practice, my players wandered around in a daze. They let pop flies drop between them and swung two beats too late at fastballs that were out of the strike zone. What's worse, they daydreamed in class and wandered the halls with their heads down, acting beaten.

In the first two weeks of the 1999 season, we had two games. The final score of the first was 15 to 1. The second one was a shutout: 15 to 0. Our team did not have the 15. I was furious after those two losses, not because we were defeated but because of the attitude of my players. They were laughing and screwing around in the dugout during the game, and doing the same on the bus on the way back to the school. "We lost," their actions screamed. "So what? It's no big deal."

I needed to get these kids on track. And fast.

On a late afternoon at the beginning of March, I gathered my players near the left field stands. I sat them down in the grass near the little hut where we stored our gear. We'd just finished practicing and we had dragged the irrigation pipes onto the field for watering. I stood there quietly for a minute. We all watched the hissing streams of water shoot from the pipe holes on the other side, showering the green blades of grass in droplets of spray.

I was flabbergasted. I didn't know what to do. So I walked down the third base line to home plate. I stood on that five-sided slab and said a prayer. "Dear God, what can I do to help these kids? How can I get them to dream? How can I push them without breaking them? How can I get them to see that there are dreams outside of their limited scope of what they think they can do?"

The answer was simple. "Go teach them what your grandfather taught you."

I walked back along the left field line in front of the stands and stood before my players. They were looking at the ground, looking off in the distance, looking at anything but me. And I just start talking.

"The thing that worries me is that I can't shake you guys from this lackadaisical attitude," I began. "I don't know if it's me; maybe I'm doing something wrong and I can't reach you. Or maybe it's you. Or maybe it's a combination."

I got their attention.

"What you better start realizing is that it takes dreams to accomplish anything. You have to have dreams. Without dreams, you're nothing in this world. You need them. And the bigger your dreams, the more you can accomplish, the more you can do."

I didn't know where this was coming from. I just opened my mouth and let the words rush out, hearing them for the first time as they were spoken. It was a little like my speaking engagements today. I never know from where the word flow springs. It's like the spirit possesses me.

"You guys have to have dreams. If you don't have dreams, you are not going to go anywhere. You have got to be educated, and you have got to have goals.

"You've got to have a ladder of success, and each time you reach one rung, you've got to add another and another and another until you go further than anybody ever thought you could. Don't let yourselves get boxed-in or put down by anybody. That's how you get better, no matter what you do in life."

I stood there for about twenty minutes and discharged every piece of wisdom I could remember from my grandfather. I thought I sounded pretty good. I should've written it all down. When I had finished there was silence. The calm seemed endless. That is until Joel DelaGarza, my senior catcher and chemistry aide, unceremoniously broke the stillness.

"What about you, coach?" he said. "You're preaching one thing and doing another."

He had my attention. I looked at the other faces wondering where this was going.

"Don't get me wrong," he said. "We all love you a lot. But the way you throw a baseball—why aren't you still playing?"

"Yeah, what are your dreams, Coach?" another player asked.

I laughed, but not at them. It was a laugh of embarrassment. I could feel my face flush with red. What they had said had nothing to do with my arm and everything to do with how they felt about me. They were naively seeing me as better than I really was.

"My dream is to watch you guys have a great season, do great in the classroom, graduate from high school, and go to college," I said.

"Well, that's funny," another one of them piped up. "Because we think you still want to play baseball."

By this point, I'd had nine surgeries and weighed about 260 pounds. My players' moms prepared meals to take with us every time we boarded the bus—homemade tortillas cooked in lard. I looked like a baseball scout, not a baseball player.

"Coach, the way you teach us the game, we know your heart's still in it," another one of them said. "When you throw to us at batting practice, we can't hit it."

"That's because you can't hit," I joked.

"What if, Coach, we start winning? Will you tryout again?" another blurted out.

"I can't do that." I responded. And I listed every reason under the sun, from weight, to age, to surgeries, to my wife and kids. At the age of twenty-eight, I had a surgery where the doctor removed 85 percent of the muscle in my shoulder. He told me I would never throw again. No, I'm not playing. Impossible. Can't be done.

"So, Coach, what if we win a district championship?" another player piped up.

Those kids couldn't remember the last time Reagan County High School had won a baseball championship of any kind.

"Coach, if we win a baseball championship, you gotta tryout again," another responded.

I argued why I should never step onto a professional pitcher's mound ever again in my life. I included the very words from the doctor who sliced up my shoulder: "It can't be done. It is impossible." At the end of ten minutes, I did what every parent in this country does when arguing with his or her kid.

I caved.

"If you guys win the district championship, I will find a Major League tryout somewhere," I promised. In the back of my mind, I was thinking two things: one, your wife will kill you; and two, it will be embarrassing. Then a third thought popped into my head: with a record of no wins and a pair of blowout losses, a district championship is a long shot. I'm not going to have to make good on this bet and make a fool of myself. I can keep eating those tortillas.

If they exceeded my expectations, which I sincerely hoped they would, I wouldn't be able to do anything about the embarrassment part. But I absolutely could not tell my wife.

So I didn't. The only people who knew about this bet were my players, my eight-year-old son, Hunter, and my dad.

"Son, even at thirty-five you're not very bright, are you," my dad said when I told him.

After that pivotal day, a funny thing happened. We started winning. By a lot. It was like a cascade. They weren't the best ballplayers in our league, but they believed in themselves and they were determined. And if you can believe in yourselves and believe in each other, you can go a long way.

I've seen a lot of really, really good players who actually sucked on the field because the members of the team didn't believe in each other. They didn't hold each other up and have each other's back. Without that level of trust, you can't project a unified front to the opposing team.

Those kids needed reinforcement and to know that I was going to be there for them no matter what. They needed to know that I expected them to do things the right way and to look and act like a cohesive unit until we actually played like a well-oiled machine without even thinking about it. Fake it 'till you make it.

Two of the losses we had later in the season were because they got cocky, not because they were lackadaisical as in those earlier losses. We had lost our humble. But those losses made them mad. It got them to thinking. It set off a fire in their bellies. That's 80 percent of success right there: figuring out where you went wrong and coming up with solutions to fuel the determination to do better. The other 20 percent is believing in yourself.

≈

The last game of our 1999 season was against the Van Horn High School Eagles—a clash of raptors for the district championship. Van Horn is a town about 250 miles west of Big Lake and the westernmost incorporated community in the vast central time zone of Texas. It was a setting for the 1989 TV miniseries *Lonesome Dove*. In 2005, Amazon founder Jeff Bezos acquired 290,000 acres just north of Van Horn to house his space tourism company, Blue Origin. In April 2018, the company launched the New Shepard suborbital capsule from the site.

But two decades earlier, the baseball clash with Van Horn would re-launch my baseball career, and forever change the course of my life. Van Horn had an ace pitcher, a kid with a nasty slider to compliment a blazing fastball. The game was played halfway between Big Lake and Van Horn on a field in Fort Stockton, home to the 7.7-mile Bridgestone/Firestone test track.

It was blistering there, even at 6 p.m., and the low-hanging sun cast a brutal glare to players on the right side. Through the first few innings, we could not hit the ball at all.

Their players swung late at our pitcher's fastball and hit an unusual number of pop-ups and ground balls to our second baseman, Joaquin. He would have normally fielded every one of them without breaking a sweat. But the mitt he had used since little league crumbled the day before, and he was using a brand new one that wasn't broken-in. His ham-fisted fielding cost us three runs.

We were behind 3 to 1 at the top of the fifth. I noticed something in their pitcher's delivery that signaled he was tiring. I told my players to be aggressive with their bats. Our first two batters singled, and our error-prone second baseman batted them home with a double. Now we were tied. We followed that with a bunt single, a triple off the right field wall, a double, and three more hits. We scored seven runs that inning. The score was now 8–3.

By the bottom of the seventh inning, the sun slipped below the horizon and the stadium lights were lit. Van Horn had logged two outs when their batter hit a pop-up to second base. Joaquin pulled it out of the air with two hands. My players rapidly converged in a heap on the mound. You'd of thought we had won the World Series. They jumped and screamed, "We did it!"

They cried through their excited joy. They hugged each other. They hugged the trophy. They hugged their parents. It was one of the best sights I've ever seen in my life.

I hung back in the dugout, snapped off a couple of rolls of Kodak moments—the digital phone-camera age being in its infancy—and savored the moment. I walked out and leaned up against the backstop thinking, "I am a pretty good coach." The thought that I now had to make good on a crazy bet never entered my mind. But I did remember that I was also the bus driver. "I'd better go start it up," I said to myself.

The thought that *did* enter my mind, as I sat in the driver's seat on our bus waiting for my players to exit the locker room, was that I wouldn't be their coach next year. The animosity between Simpson and me had come to a poisonous head. Though the Reagan County High School principal had asked me to remain on as a science teacher in the fall, Simpson had already hired my coaching replacement. Staying on just to teach would have been too painful to endure.

I had a job lined up in Fort Worth at Eastern Hills High—a 4-A school—as a football coach and head baseball coach. I sat in the bus and called newspaper and TV reporters in and around Big Lake letting them know the Owls had won the district championship. I looked out the window and saw my players still celebrating an achievement that not even they themselves thought they could accomplish.

That's when I realized that everything was about them. It was about every kid I coached and every student in every classroom I taught. I discovered I was crying, weeping over something other than myself. I tell people I was crying because I was thirty-five and my gut was expanding, and I was losing my hair. But, in reality, I got really sentimental over these kids. Their growth and achievement touched me deeply. They meant a whole lot to me.

As I was sitting there shedding tears, Joaquin, my second baseman, hopped up to the top step of the bus. He was a tough kid who was absolutely the last player on the team who needed to see me sobbing. He giggled.

"Shut up," I said.

Then he stuck out his hand and presented me with a baseball. On it was written, "Reagan County Owls District 1 AA Champs 1999." Every player had signed it. I started crying harder—a big fat coach slobbering in the front seat of the bus. Great. As Joaquin walked by, he patted me on the shoulder.

"We did our part Coach. Now it's your turn," he said.

I turned and waved. "I gotcha...oh my God." That's when I remembered the bet. At the beginning of the season, these kids couldn't hit anything I threw at them. By the end of the season, I had a tough time getting them out. Now I was supposed to impress a Major League scout? Every kid boarding the bus told me the same thing.

"Our part of the bargain is done. Now you do your part."

"You gotta try out now."

"A deal's a deal."

"We did it. You have to, too."

"Okay," I said. "I get it."

I'm going to get laughed off the planet, I thought to myself. But I knew if I was to have any credibility with these kids, I had to keep my word.

For the next four hours, I drove that bus home, deep in thought. One of those thoughts was: *your wife is going to kill you*. So I didn't tell her. Embarrassing myself would be good enough. I didn't need to let everybody in on the upcoming humiliation.

The following week, we got knocked out of the playoffs in a best of three series. We won the first game, lost the second in the bottom of the seventh, and fell apart completely in the third game. Our championship season had come to an end. My season of likely disgrace, or unlikely triumph, had begun.

At the conclusion of the series, my players hugged me and told me how happy they were to play for me. I was deeply honored to coach them, and heartened to see them thrive.

⁓

It was the last day of school. I had all of my teaching materials packed into my red Ford Ranger pickup. That truck was a beater. It had a five-speed manual transmission and no air conditioning, power steering, or power brakes. It was 110 degrees that day, so I had to make the seventy-mile trip back to San Angelo with the windows down.

My headphones were plugged into a little cassette player I had resting on the seat. The country song "Somebody's Out There Watching" by the Kinleys piped into my ears. That song was the first single released from *Touched by an Angel: The Album*, the soundtrack to the popular TV series at the time of the same name. I was looking forward to a fresh start after spending two years focusing only on teaching, coaching, and parenting.

But I was torn. I didn't know what I was supposed to do, what path I was supposed to pursue. I had a good job lined up at Eastern Hills High School in Fort Worth, and I had this baseball dream I somehow got sidetracked into chasing. Should I choose the safe route, or should I throw caution to the gritty West Texas breeze and tryout for a Major League

Baseball team? I had to talk to God. I parked, got out of my truck, and sat on the hood. The heat of the dull painted metal cooked through the denim of my jeans and warmed my skin into a feverish burn.

I began to pray, plead really. "God, I am stubborn and I am hard headed and I honestly don't know what I'm supposed to do. You're going to have to show me the way. I've got this job in Fort Worth. Is that what I'm supposed to do? I've got this tryout I've committed myself to. But base-ball is really not an option for me at the age of thirty-five. What is it you want me to do? Please show me the way."

I got back into my truck and headed down Highway 67, the desolate scrub and road kill barely registering a blip in my awareness. I was looking, listening for some sign, some hint as to what God wanted me to do.

Not long after I got home, I found a tryout at Dallas Baptist University. It was open to about 700 kids. That's a big audience to play the fool in front of. Plus, Dallas was four-and-a-half hours away, a nine-hour round trip. Since I hadn't told my wife about the bet and the kids—then ages eight, four, and one—were under my care on Saturday's while she worked, this would be a tough absence to explain.

Then my dad called. He read an announcement in the local newspaper to me over the phone. The Tampa Bay Devil Rays were having a tryout at Howard Payne University in Brownwood on June 19, 1999. The first sixty or seventy kids to get there would have the opportunity to tryout.

"You'd better get there early," he said, "because they're going to count you twice." It was his way of jokingly driving home the point that I was twice the age of these potential young prospects.

Brownwood was just an hour and ten minutes from San Angelo, and our absence would have a built-in explanation. I jumped on it. When that Saturday arrived, my wife was getting ready for work. I was sitting around the breakfast table with the kids.

"What are you and the kids going to go do today?" she asked.

"We're going to go see grandpa," my four-year-old daughter Jessica yelled.

You see, this wasn't really a lie. It's what we actually did. At worst it was a fib by omission. My dad had agreed to watch the kids while I wound up and threw a few fastballs. So, I packed the kids into the Ranger and we were off.

When we arrived at Howard Payne, I parked the Ranger down by the left field line. I watched those hopeful kids get out of their cars, smiling from ear-to-ear. They were tall, thin, and athletic with brand new bodies and brand new gear. I looked down at the gut hanging over the elastic band of my softball pants. Thankfully, this detail was not depicted in the movie thanks to the svelte physique of Dennis Quaid. "Wow. What have I done?" I whispered to myself.

My son Hunter must have sensed my hesitation. He gave me a hard stare.

"You made a promise," he said. "It's time to get out there."

"You're going to walk home is what you're going to do," I said. He giggled.

I approached the sign-up table lugging a diaper bag with three kids in tow. The kid in front of me signed up and walked off. The scout looked up at me.

"How many kids did you bring?" he said. That scout was about sixty-five. His name was Doug Gassaway.

"Three," I said.

"No, to tryout?"

"Let me explain something," I said. "I made a promise to a group of kids I coached on a baseball team, kids who do not believe in adults. I promised them that if they did something nobody thought they could do, I'd do something I know I can't do. It's going to be embarrassing, maybe even humiliating. But you'll get a great laugh out of it. So, if you'll just let me throw, I can go home and tell my players I lived up to my end of the deal."

He shook his head and tapped his pen on the table. "All right," he said. "I'll let you throw but you're going to throw last. These kids are here for serious business. They have to throw from the outfield. They have to hit. They're going to be timed in the sixty-yard run. Do you want to run?"

"I don't run," I said.

When I was done filling out the paperwork, Gassaway looked up and gave me a hard stare, an unsmiling expression.

"Son, why didn't you just shave your head like every other coach in America?"

When I finished my business at the sign-up table, I noticed all of these young kids warming up, throwing the ball to each other. But no one would play catch with me. I was too old. So for the next four-and-a-half hours, the kids and I had a picnic with my dad. We played games. I changed diapers. It was a windy day and we all got sunburned. Then, after everybody had tried out, Gassaway called me up and handed me a baseball.

"Do you need to warm up?" he asked.

"What, to embarrass myself? No. I would just like to pitch quickly, run off the field, and hope to remember to grab my kids on the way to the car."

Gassaway laughed, walked back behind the screen, and picked up the radar gun.

"Anytime you're ready," he said.

The kid who was catching for me had just turned nineteen the day of the tryout. He had graduated two weeks before. He gave me a sign for a fastball. I wound up and released the ball through my fingers, throwing as hard as I possibly could. I thought it was a great pitch. I looked over the catcher's head behind the screen and saw Gassaway shaking the radar gun. *Wow. I didn't even throw hard enough to register on the gun*, I thought to myself. Gassaway called for another gun to verify his readings. Now there are two guns measuring my pitching speed.

"Keep throwing," Gassaway commanded.

I kept unleashing pitches. I was sweating. I felt aches and pains burning across my arm. All of the young kids before me had thrown around twenty pitches. My pitch count was escalating toward fifty and then sixty. "What the hell?" I whispered to myself.

The kids who had tried out before were now loading their bags and equipment into their cars. And I'm up there on the mound throwing and throwing and throwing. Sweat drip streams were stinging my eyes and tracing salty stripes against my cheeks.

All of a sudden, those kids who were loading their baseball wares into their escape vehicles were beginning to congregate around the screen. Gassaway fixed his eyes on one of them.

"Hey, grab a bat and get into the box," he said.

"You want me to get in there with that?" the kid said.

That's when it hit me. Maybe I'm not doing as bad as I thought.

When this grueling torture test on the mound concluded, I gathered up my kids and headed for the truck. They'd been in the hot sun all day, their skin rosy red. Jaimee was crying as I loaded them into the Ranger. I turned the fan on high. The kid who was catching my pitches approached the driver's side of my truck.

"Sir, you threw better than anybody today," he says.

"That's because nobody here can throw," I deadpanned.

"No. You had them talking back there."

"I'm sure I did. Thank you."

He wished me luck and ran off. Then Gassaway approached.

"I remember you," he says. "Fifteen years ago at Ranger Junior College you were a football star. Everybody wanted to make a pitcher out of you."

"Yes sir."

"Jimmy, back then you were tall and thin and threw eighty-seven or eighty-eight."

"Yes sir."

"Well son, I don't know what you've done in your time off. But the first pitch you threw without warming up was ninety-four. Everything after that was ninety-eight. Look, you're old, but you throw ninety-eight and you're left-handed. I've got to call it in. And if I don't, you could sign with someone else and I'll get fired. They're going to think I'm crazy, but you might get a phone call."

When you're an old man, and you find out you're throwing ninety-eight, there is a happy dance going on in your head. But when you're an educator and you find out you've been throwing 98 miles an hour at high school kids, you might get sued. That discovery was a mixed blessing.

I later found out that, at one point, Gassaway had a drinking problem. So when he called in to say that he had a thirty-five-year-old lefty that threw fastballs at 98 miles per hour, they thought he was hitting the sauce again.

"Don't be surprised if you get a phone call," he repeated.

But it wasn't one phone call. It was twelve. When we first got home, Lorri was dropping the phone handset into the cradle. She turned around.

"So, where have we been today?"

My oldest daughter Jessica had a hold of my leg. She looked at Lorri.

"We're not supposed to tell you," she said in a singsong voice.

"What were you thinking?" was my wife's perturbed response. "What are you going to do now?"

"I'm going to do the right thing," I said. "I've got that job in Fort Worth and the opportunity to work with more kids in a bigger environment. I'm good at that. I love that."

"Well then you'd better listen to these phone messages," she said. One was from the director of scouting for the Devil Rays.

"We heard you threw pretty good today," he said. "We would like you to come back and throw again in two days at

Howard Payne. Our scouts are going to be there, and we'll see if you can throw that hard or if your arm falls off."

I called my high school players and told them the news.

"If I do good here, they want me to sign a contract," I announced.

"Well then let's go," they said. They followed me to Brownwood for my second trial by fire, seeing to it that I followed through on my word.

Only there wasn't any fire. There was a flood. The sky was bursting at the seams, unleashing a torrent. Lightening ripped through the fabric of the heavens. Thunder shuddered the ground. My kids and I plowed through the storm to Brownwood and Howard Payne University where I was to attempt a repeat performance. Half my baseball team showed up.

There were no other kids waiting in the wings to endure this trial, so the head coach of the Howard Payne baseball team took on the role of designated catcher. The rain was so heavy by this time, they handed me a new ball before for every pitch. I was sliding in mud up to my knee after every throw.

My pitches streaked across the plate with such ferocity that the catcher misjudged almost every one. He just couldn't catch the ball. Some pitches hit him in the chest padding. Others struck him in the foot. I was throwing 98-mile-an-hour fastballs, and 91-mile-an-hour sliders.

I unleashed eighty pitches through that muddy cloudburst. When I had finished, the Devil Rays scout said the team wanted me to sign a contract. It was minor league agreement, which meant I would have to take a big pay cut from teaching and coaching. I talked the offer over with my team.

"Coach, you told us that if we ever had our dream in front of us that we should chase it no matter what," they said. "You don't look back. You don't look around. You go."

"I was lying," I said defensively.

I signed the contract.

Twelve weeks later I was on the mound facing the Texas Rangers at the Ballpark at Arlington. I had achieved a dream I had nurtured since I was barely more than a toddler. All because of a group of kids who, when I pushed them to be the best they could be, pushed the same back on me.

Oftentimes, when you set out to inspire people to grow beyond their field of perceived possibilities, you don't know who is actually mentoring whom—for whom the whole drama is unfolding. If you think you're in charge, if you think you're the one doing the motivating and the influencing, that's when reality slaps you in the face. Hard. It's also when the magic happens. It's when dreams come true.

It's hard to grapple with how unlikely my ascent to the Major League mound actually was. I was thirty-five years old. My fastball never clocked more than 88 miles per hour when I was in my early twenties. My shoulder had been carved up like a ham hock.

Then, suddenly, at the age of thirty-five, I was throwing 98-mile-per-hour fastballs and 91-mile-per-hour sliders. That simply doesn't happen. Not in this world. Not in the normal course of things. It was a miracle. I credit God. And those blessed kids.

CHAPTER 8

JOURNEY THROUGH PAIN

As I travel the country and tell my story, I've come to believe that I'm fulfilling a divine purpose. In a world full of spin, Photoshop retouching, and endless edits, my story is ugly, full of incisions, stitches, scars, and pain. Sometimes we want to turn and look away from that reality, from that pain. We want everything to look good, to be easy, to be comfortable. We want life to resemble the sitcom stories we see on TV, and the feel-good dramas and romcoms we take in at the Cineplex. Pass the popcorn.

But it's in the middle of our struggles with pain where we learn the power of faith. It's through these trials we begin to experience the fullness of life. It's in these trying depths where we best learn who we are.

I am one of those rare people who doesn't know when to quit. Call it stubbornness or steel resolve, but if someone told me I couldn't do something, I was bound and determined to show them that I could. I didn't quit playing football when I separated my shoulder. I didn't drop out of the game after suffering a series of concussions. It took several surgeries to force me to quit baseball the first time. Most people give up when life gets hard. I quit way past the point where the sloping line of the bell curve normally terminates. It's all or nothing with me. There is no in-between.

I distinctly remember one game where I played outfield on a softball team while in college. A fly ball was hit over my head and I was determined to catch it. I knew the outfield wall was close, but I wanted that ball. That's all that mattered. I slammed into the wall with my whole body, breaking a toe and suffering a concussion in the process. But I caught the ball.

I've always competed against *me* first. I pushed my body to extremes to see just how good I could become. I stressed my muscles, tendons, and bones to their absolute limits. I pushed myself to prove my dad wrong.

What does the best Jimmy Morris look like?

How hard can the best Jimmy Morris throw?

Is Jimmy Morris really good enough?

When I played football, I wanted to crucify my opponents. I wanted to crush them. With my head. Like a missile. I thought I was invincible. I broke bones and suffered *dozens* of concussions playing with all my heart, trying to be a better me. Pain, to me, is just one more thing to overcome—another challenge.

In football, I learned not to kick off a ball and watch how far it goes because someone's going to hit you in the ear hole if you do. Then you get up and your helmet's facing one way and your head is facing the other.

Today, there's not a day that goes by that I'm not in pain. I'm in pain right now as I write this. When I'm doing things, I can tune it out and complete the task at hand. Compete in a sport. Talk to people. Get into the car and drive for five hours to a destination. Pain comes and goes. The way people adapt to it makes them who they are. There have been precious few times in my life when I thought I couldn't take the pain anymore.

Most of the time I just think, *we're going to get through this*. You move on. You overcome. You persevere. It's just another obstacle.

⌖

My journey through pain began at birth. When I came into this world on January 19, 1964, I weighed in at nearly ten pounds. That hefty weight prepared me for my first health scare. Thirty-six hours after my birth, I was diagnosed with pneumonia and was put in isolation for the next ten days. This ordeal, which very nearly killed me, left me with weak lungs and severe asthma.

As I grew, my asthma attacks would sometimes get so bad that I came close to death. These attacks would be followed by pneumonia within twenty-four hours. Doctors had warned my parents for years to not allow me to play baseball, football, or roughhouse on grass. The allergens in the grass were known to incite asthma attacks. They considered it a matter of life and death. One thing's for sure: I considered it death if I couldn't play sports or spar outside.

In my early teens, I came home after one game and went straight to bed. I didn't want anything to eat, not even the porterhouse steak my mother prepared for dinner. I gasped for air. I was incapable of drawing any breath at all. My mom and dad rushed me to the hospital.

The first epinephrine shot they gave me in the emergency room did nothing. The second did little. Twelve epinephrine shots later and I was still wheezing and struggling for breath. So, they hooked me up to an IV and an oxygen mask. I remained in the hospital like that for five days.

Outside of normal scrapes and blows, that was the most dramatic health crisis I experienced during my childhood. At the age of seven, I fell out of a tree after a bunch of kids targeted me with rocks, attempting to knock me out of my perch in the high branches. I broke my arm and suffered a concussion. The doctors weren't concerned about the concussion. They treated my arm, the more obvious issue. It was the first of many serious head blows I would suffer in my childhood and through adolescence.

A month after Brownwood High School won the Texas state football championship, I was involved in a severe car accident. A couple of grandparents traveling in a car with their grandson ran through a stop sign and T-boned my pickup. There was a house with a tall fence, just before the intersection, that blocked my view. I had the right of way and I didn't see them coming. By the time I cleared that fence they were already out into the intersection. They couldn't stop. They hit me broadside at 55 miles per hour on the passenger side of the truck.

I had a seatbelt on, but no shoulder strap and my head punched a hole through the windshield. The next thing I know, I'm rolling backwards down the road the other way. The impact literally tore the bed off my pickup. I had the Eagles playing full blast on the car radio. The only thing that worked on that truck after impact was the Eagles. They were still playing while I rolled down the road backwards. The grandpa, grandma, and grandson escaped injury.

Probably the only thing that saved me was all of the conditioning and training I went through in football practice to strengthen my neck. Otherwise, I'm sure it would have snapped. I spent a few days in the hospital recovering. Back then, they didn't dispense pain pills like they do now. I gritted my teeth and clenched my fists to get through the torment. I believe that accident severely impacted my health three decades later.

∽

I remember various events in recent history by recalling a corresponding surgery or health crisis. I had staples in my arm when the Space Shuttle Challenger exploded. I had my gall bladder removed shortly after Osama bin Laden was killed. The Boston Marathon bombing happened on April 15, 2013. Two days later I was diagnosed with Parkinson's disease.

I underwent my very first surgery at the age of twenty-one, on the night before I was slated to pitch the opening day game in rookie ball. My trainer rushed me to the hospital for an emergency appendectomy. That night, in less than an hour, my temperature soared from normal to 104. I was in the hospital for four days.

After that surgery, doctors instructed me to take it easy, to rest. I was told not to throw or do anything physically demanding. But because I had accumulated so much wisdom by the age of twenty-one, I felt I knew better than the doctors. I convinced one of my friends to play catch with me at my apartment.

I got caught. I was sent home for two weeks and given strict orders to focus on healing. After those two weeks, I went to Arizona to train and get back in game-day shape. I exercised hard. I practiced with rigor and passion. I started pitching again and did exceptionally well, earning my first promotion to Class-A ball.

After pitching a game in 1986, I woke up in pain. My roommate, lefthander Dan Plesac who went on to pitch for the Milwaukee Brewers, got a hold of my wrist and attempted to straighten my left arm. The pain was excruciating. My arm was purple from the wrist to the shoulder. There was a huge knot in my elbow. That's when I had my first "Tommy John" surgery, or ulnar collateral ligament reconstruction.

Throwing overhand goes against everything—anatomy-wise—the human body was designed for. Repetitive throwing motion puts a lot of tension on the ulnar collateral ligament in the medial elbow, causing it to stretch, fray, and tear. To relieve it, orthopedic surgeon Frank Jobe removed a tendon from my heel and grafted it into my elbow.

When I awoke from surgery, my leg hurt worse than my elbow did. Not only that, I noticed that someone had tied a yellow ribbon around my member. I was horrified to say the least. I don't know who did it (a nurse?), when they did it, how many people knew about it, or if they took Polaroids. But there it was, a symbolic strip of yellow around my manhood.

I was out of baseball for more than eight months after that surgery. But when I came back, I was hurling my fastball at 90 miles per hour. Whether or not this was the result of the surgery, or of the affixed yellow ribbon, remains a mystery to this day.

My second comeback began during fall ball in 1986, a period when Desmond Tutu became the first black bishop for the Anglican Church in South Africa, *The Oprah Winfrey Show* was syndicated, and the Red Sox came close to winning their first World Series championship since 1918. My fall ball season was strong, and I was excited about my playing opportunities for the next year.

I exercised hard in the off-season so I could be "in the best shape of my life." At spring training in 1987, my hopes were high. *I could break camp with the Double-A team,* I thought. *This is my year.*

But it wasn't to be. I had focused so much on getting my elbow back into shape during the off-season that I neglected to properly develop and condition my shoulder. During spring training, my shoulder went out. That spurred my first shoulder surgery.

I was out of baseball for another year.

In 1989, George H. W. Bush was in the White House and I was again in good shape, playing with the White Sox in spring training. And then I came down with the flu. I broke camp, not a step closer to the majors, but back in Class-A ball. I was absolutely furious. I had only pitched in two games and, yet again, my elbow was killing me. Not only that, my heart was no longer in the game. I wanted to throw in the towel. I was ready to go home. I was convinced that this dream I had been keeping alive since I was a little kid was not for me. I gave up on *me.*

I gave up on baseball the first time because I couldn't stay healthy. Yet if I had achieved my baseball dream at the age of twenty-one, I know I would have been an insufferable spoiled brat. My grandparents taught me well, but they couldn't erase the fifteen years I spent being raised by dysfunctional parents or the fifteen-year nightmare I'd endured with my father. It took another fifteen years of ups, downs, struggles, and pain before God opened the doors to my dream once more.

◆

In the two decades after I retired from Major League Baseball, I had more than forty surgeries. They were performed to relieve pain, to remedy digestive system issues, and to treat nerve and bone injuries. I had a nerve go bad in my leg, a condition diagnosed as "nerve entrapment." Doctors went in and released the nerve. Four months later, another nerve condition popped up and I had another surgery to release that nerve, and then another. And another. It was a ridiculous and endless cycle. My body was falling apart, and my doctors hadn't the slightest idea why.

I was averaging two-and-a-half surgeries a year, so I was on pain pills for close to two decades. Starting in 2000, when I was with the Devil Rays and in-between these surgeries, I was afflicted with headaches—pounding, skull-splitting headaches of unbelievable intensity. It was like a vice was clamped to my temples and the handle was slowly being turned until the throbbing hit the perfect pulse cadence to maximize pain. I could easily visualize a sadistic dungeon master behind my suffering.

These headaches would follow a predictable pattern: I'd get a sinus infection, my neck would lock up, and the headaches would build momentum and then slam into my skull like a freight train. Sometimes these headaches would last for six months. My doctors were baffled. They thought I had an autoimmune disorder.

To give me some semblance of relief, my doctors prescribed stronger pain pills. When that didn't work, I said to myself, "You know what? I think I'll have a slug of vodka on top of that so I can get some of this pain to go away." As time went on, those slugs got bigger and bigger. It was a recurring cycle of crap.

In addition to the headaches, I suffered from tremors, insomnia, horrible nightmares, and extreme physical movement during sleep. I stopped swinging my arms when I walked, and gradually lost my ability to make facial expressions. I was constantly fatigued, and began speaking rapidly and more softly—awesome when you are a motivational speaker. Not. I also experienced non-stop nerve pain all over my body. These symptoms were followed by loss of my sense of taste and smell.

In the spring of 2010, I suffered from neck and shoulder pain. In an attempt to outwit my own brain, I exercised constantly. I believed working out hard and being sore from exertion was better than sitting in pain. Why not create my own pain through exercise? That way my brain doesn't know if the pain is due to exercise soreness or something else. That way, I had at least some control. Keep moving and living… or sitting and dying.

While lifting weights, I noticed my fingers going numb and sharp tingles danced from my fingertips and down along the joints. I was diagnosed with thoracic outlet syndrome, a condition that occurs when the blood vessels and nerves in between the collarbone and the first rib of the rib cage become compressed.

After multiple nerve conduction tests, a thoracic outlet specialist confirmed the damage. In May of that year, I underwent thoracic outlet surgery, a treatment that has become much more common among Major League Baseball pitchers over the last few years. The procedure calls for the removal of that first rib.

Shawna initially thought it would be funny to keep the rib, but it was actually pretty disgusting. So we threw it away. To this day, the only ribs I like are those slathered in barbecue sauce with a side of fries and chased down by a Dr. Pepper. We usually throw those away too, but only after we've sucked them dry of their meaty, spicy, and tangy goodness.

On April 17, 2013, I was diagnosed with chronic traumatic encephalopathy (CTE)-induced Parkinsonism, the result of a long series of concussions from sports injuries. The diagnosis came after a DaTSCAN, a diagnostic method that uses a radioactive isotope that's injected into the body and binds to dopamine transporters in the brain. The signal from the isotope is then detected by special gamma cameras. My test showed I was lacking dopamine on the right side of my brain.

At first, we tried fighting the disease through a medication regimen. Doctors prescribed Sentimet, a Carbidopa/Levodopa mix, to minimize the tremors and other symptoms, but it made me nauseated. I was always sick to my stomach and it got worse with each passing day. It got to the point where I couldn't eat anything and had trouble keeping down what little I forced myself to consume.

In search of relief, I played the doctor shuffle game, going from physician to physician. I could barely keep straight which doctors I was seeing and when I was supposed to see them. I was at the end of my rope when I contacted a neurosurgeon, who suggested I explore deep brain stimulation (DBS) surgery. In DBS treatment, a neurostimulator embedded in the chest sends electrical impulses to electrodes implanted in specific areas of the brain to counteract Parkinson's symptoms. We went over the pros and cons of the treatment.

"There is always risk in surgery, one of the biggest is that you might lose your voice over time," the surgeon said. He had patients whose voice was reduced to a low whisper.

"That's a pretty substantial risk for a motivational speaker," I argued. But I plunged ahead, desperate for relief; I was desperate to get my life back.

The surgeon wanted written approval from the doctor who'd initially determined the Parkinson's diagnoses, but he wasn't cooperative. He wasn't convinced this treatment was the correct course of action. He wanted to keep playing with my brain chemistry. But I knew that wasn't the solution. I was reacting badly to the drugs. I was living a shell of a life. I just wanted the pain and debilitation to stop.

"You are the one who hired that doctor," a friend advised me. "You can fire him."

So I did. I fired the diagnosing doctor and went ahead with the surgery, eighteen months after my diagnosis.

I was actually awake for the first part of the procedure. The surgeon attached a metal cage around my head, somewhat like a dog's "cone of shame." The cage was placed to keep my head perfectly still while they positioned the electrodes. Then they administered the real drugs and knocked me out. They woke me during different phases to test my ability to speak, move my arms, legs, etc.

On the day of my surgery the hospital was overbooked, so I laid in recovery for eight hours until my room became available. I could overhear the conversations among the nurses and patients, though I couldn't yet open my eyes. I heard the woman next to me say that she needed to use the restroom. The nurse brought her a bedpan.

And then I smelled pee. There's nothing like the pungent smell of pee to propel someone through the effects of anesthesia. It's like olfactory jet fuel. It had been years since I could smell anything. I couldn't remember the last scents I could positively identify. I was even immune to my black lab's room-clearing gas. I had quit cooking—something I once loved to do—because my ability to taste went dead and I couldn't tell if what I was preparing was edible. At the time, I didn't know the loss of taste and smell was an early indicator of Parkinson's.

While I was still in recovery, Shawna came to sit with me and once we had our own room, she brought in Italian food. I got a whiff of it and it smelled fantastic. I didn't tell her. I didn't know if it would last.

Even though the doctors wouldn't turn on the device until two weeks after surgery, I felt great. The electrodes themselves were therapeutic even before they carried a current. This was called the honeymoon phase.

I could smell, I could taste, and I had balance.

I could even fasten the buttons on my shirt.

Most importantly, I could still talk.

To this day, Shawna will swear she knew I would never lose my voice. From the moment we first considered the DBS option, she was convinced God would preserve my voice. On the way home from DBS surgery, I felt so good I asked her to stop at a dealership so that we could look at new trucks. The next day we bought one: a black GMC Sierra. Purebred Detroit iron. Sweet ride.

The symptoms of Parkinson's were gone.

All except for the pain, that is.

༺ঞ༻

I've been told that Parkinson's attacks at a cellular level, and from my experience, the pain does too. Initially, my doctors insisted that Parkinson's doesn't cause pain. They implied it was all in my head. But after multiple visits and after they reviewed the research, they discovered that over 80 percent of those diagnosed with Parkinson's describe increased pain as a symptom.

In April of 2015, I was invited to speak at a Michael J. Fox Foundation event at The Ballpark in Arlington. Afterwards, I visited with several people suffering from Parkinson's who told me that pain was also their primary experience with the disease.

Finally, I knew I wasn't crazy. I wasn't alone in battling this disease or the horrific pain. Just hearing from others who had similar experiences to mine was a big relief. The magnetic resonance imaging procedures I underwent after complaining of severe headaches showed scarring in areas of my brain where I had reported head pain. So I know my headaches weren't psychosomatic, or a figment of my imagination.

In January of 2016, I was diagnosed with gastroparesis, yet another symptom of Parkinson's. Gastroparesis is a medical disorder characterized by the partial paralysis of the stomach muscles. Food remains in the stomach for prolonged periods and isn't moved through the digestive system.

Food took forever to digest, and my stomach was forcing it in the wrong direction. I was nauseous all the time, as food would literally rot in my stomach. Pleasant to imagine, I know. Plus, my medications gave me severe acid reflux and it was destroying my esophagus. To relieve the condition, I had gastric bypass surgery. It worked. I now have a thumb-sized pouch at the end of my esophagus I lovingly call a "thumbach."

Still, the pain persisted.

I began experiencing severe back pain and my left leg started to drag when I walked. Desperate for help, Shawna called Wanda, her spiritual mom.

"Let me pray and I will call you back," she said. When Wanda called back, she told Shawna to put her index finger on the back of my neck while she continued to pray.

"It's his back, it's his back," Shawna insisted. "Not his neck."

"Keep your finger there while I'm praying," she said to Shawna. "When I see Jimmy, I see light on the back of his neck. That's the source. That's what God is showing me."

We later went to see the surgeon who performed my DBS procedure, and he conducted a full MRI scan of my spine. What they found was stunning. They discovered I was suffering from cervical spondylotic myelopathy, a condition caused by arthritic changes in the cervical vertebrae in the neck. It results in a narrowing of the spinal canal, which ultimately causes compression of the spinal cord. Another disc in my neck had gone bad, the one above my existing fusion. My neck problems were most likely due to long-ago injuries in football, and that car accident where my head punched through the windshield. The disc and bone spurs were squishing the spinal cord, preventing the spinal fluid from moving properly.

As a result, all my nerve signals were getting mixed up and my brain was sending out confused messages to the rest of my body. "Oh, you hurt your knee. Oh, you hurt your ankle. Oh, you hurt your shoulder." Because of this jumbled messaging, I was not only experiencing pain, but I was also losing my ability to walk and move my head, and the pain was only increasing. I later found out that if I had made one wrong move or had bumped my head, the disc and bone spurs could have caused irreparable damage to my spinal column, leaving me crippled for life.

On February 13, 2018, I underwent a surgical procedure to relieve the pressure. The surgeon shaved away bone material from the vertebrae to release the spinal cord, fused that disc to the others below, and put a wire cage around it to prevent it from growing back into the spinal cord.

During physical therapy after surgery, I was no longer dragging my leg. I walked with the physical therapist through the hospital hallway, reaching up to touch the doorway to give it a high five. Incredible! I was thrilled that I could walk.

Although I was still in excruciating pain, my doctor told me I would begin to feel less pain over time. The severity of the spinal cord impingement meant it would take time for my nerves to heal. Dr. Arnold Vardiman, my neurosurgeon and earthly healer, had believed me. He found the source of my pain. He thought outside of the box. I am forever grateful.

Then, one morning out of the blue, I took a look at Shawna and said, "Let's go for a walk." The pain was gone. I had my mobility back. Even more amazing, I was able to ratchet down and eventually turn off my DBS unit. I had no tremors, and no headaches. I had balance.

So—was I suffering from Parkinson's, or was it cervical myelopathy all along? It's hard to say because cervical myopathy doesn't take away your sense of smell or taste. The loss of these sensations is a definite symptom of Parkinson's.

Why did doctors keep missing this? Before this procedure, I'd had surgery on my neck to fuse the vertebra just below where cervical myelopathy was discovered. The doctor had completely missed it. How is that possible? Did it happen afterward? Yet, I had Parkinson's symptoms before that fusion. Mystery or miracle? As a person of faith, I choose the latter.

God did not cause my suffering. I did. I believe He allowed me to experience this long bout of torment because he's preparing me for something in the future. Maybe it's for a purpose I have not been let in on yet. I don't know. What I do know is that, after this long ordeal, I'm far more prepared to face the grueling challenges ahead and more able to reach out to and empathize with people in pain than I ever have been in my life.

CHAPTER 9

NAKED JUMPING JACKS: THE PRICE OF VODKA AND CRANBERRY JUICE

Following my dual diagnosis of peripheral neuropathy and Parkinson's disease in 2013, I was in constant, unrelenting pain. Even with a cache of powerful medications—Oxycodone, multiple Benzodiazepines, Lyrica, muscle relaxers, and a sleep aid—I could not get comfortable. I constantly battled with insomnia. The regimen of meds dulled my emotions a lot and my pain a little, but they also prevented the deep sleep I so desperately needed.

So I would isolate myself, especially from those who I thought could see through me. I would wake up from a light sleep at three in the morning and plant myself on the couch to write, watch TV, or color. In fact, I was a compulsive colorer. I had maybe thirty coloring books and a huge collection of coloring pens. Staying inside the lines of an image in a coloring book was the only sense of control I felt I had.

Sure, I had faith. I just didn't have faith in me. There were people around me who loved me, but I was making myself unlovable. So I kept to myself because I was my own best company. I didn't want anybody else around me, especially when I was in pain.

So out of utter despair I prescribed vodka—lots of it—to get out of this painful funk. I was downing a liter—mostly Tito's Handmade Vodka from Austin—every two days, mixing it with cranberry juice to help it go down easier (you know, because cranberry juice is good for you). I would pause my drinking long enough to successfully get through a speech. But when I was done speaking, I'd mix me a vodka and cranberry juice and pop me a pill.

In fact, I had this professional routine. I would drink on the flight to the destination where I was scheduled to speak—because airplane rides hurt bad, something about the cabin pressure, I think. When I got to the hotel, I'd order a bottle of wine and before I knew it, the bottle was empty. Then I'd get up the next day, do my speech, go to the airport, and order a Bloody Mary. On the flight home I'd sit in first class and imbibe for free—two or three drinks to wash down a couple of pain pills.

It was a dangerous pattern. I never missed or screwed up a speech because of my habit, nor did I ever suffer from hangovers. There were many times I gave some of my best speeches while in excruciating pain. There is no way to explain how, except God. He was protecting me from myself. I never upped the dosage of my meds beyond what was prescribed. So I never ran out of pills. I never ran out of vodka either. When the liquor store clerk knows you by name, maybe—just maybe—you go there too often.

I was so used to the pain and the attempts to deal with it that the routine itself became an addiction. As a result, we were constantly visiting liquor stores to acquire ever more vodka. I remember one such trip in October 2016— through streets with houses decked-out in Halloween decorations—to a nearby convenience store. Shawna drove our GMC Yukon because I was in so much pain and on meds that impaired my driving ability. It had been raining, so the streets and the parking lot pavement were wet.

Shawna waited for me in the Yukon while I went inside the store to pick up my vodka. Smirnoff was on sale and there was this merchandising display of bottles assembled into a large pyramid. It was an impressive piece of architecture.

As I reached for a bottle of Tito's from the shelf next to the display, my wet shoes slipped out from under me on the slick tile floor. I lost my balance. There was nothing solid I could grab onto to break the inevitable plunge. On my way down to the floor, I took out the whole pyramid, smashing twenty-five bottles on the floor. I hadn't even had a drink that day.

I started yelling for Shawna, but she couldn't see the slapstick scene I had created in the store from her position in the Yukon's driver's seat. So the clerk ran out to the SUV and knocked on the window to alert her. He was probably terrified we were going to sue him and the store. I was afraid I was going to have to pay for a couple of dozen bottles of vodka.

I'd already started to feel the effects of the fall after I regained my balance and got back on my feet. I knew I would be sore from the resultant cuts and bruises for days, if not weeks. Shawna was horrified. We apologized profusely. I grabbed an unbroken bottle and shuffled over to the register. "Can I just pay for this and then we'll leave?" I mumbled. I was determined to get my vodka. Addiction is very embarrassing.

My sorry habit came to a head in early November of that year, just a couple days after the Chicago Cubs won their first World Series in 108 years. Shawna and I were at San Antonio International Airport in the security line preparing to leave for a speaking engagement in Green Bay, Wisconsin. I placed my backpack on the x-ray conveyor belt and began to walk through the metal detector. While waiting for my bag to be x-rayed on the other side, I heard:

"Sir! Is this your bag?" a TSA agent asked tersely.

"Yes," I answered.

"Sir! Is this your bag?" he asked a second time, raising his voice.

"Yes, that's my bag," I said.

"Sir! Do you have a weapon in your bag?"

"No," I responded.

"Sir! Do you have a weapon in your bag?" he repeated.

"No, I don't have a weapon."

"Sir! Is this your bag or not?"

"Yes, that is my bag! No, I do not have a weapon in my bag!"

The security guard then turned the screen to face us. "Sir! Is this your weapon?"

"Oh crap!"

When we travel by car within the state of Texas, I typically carry a 9-millimeter pistol with me for protection. We were returning home from Fort Worth following our charity foundation work at O. D. Wyatt High School and the NASCAR event with Michael McDowell at Texas Motor Speedway. I'd taken the gun from the car and brought it with us into the hotel in Fort Worth, slipping it into the shoe pocket underneath the main compartment of my backpack. I believed it was safer to bring it in with us than to leave it in our unattended car. I quickly forgot about it. When we returned home from the event and repacked for Green Bay, the gun was still in my backpack.

The TSA agents photographed the screen showing the image of the handgun and took my backpack. They led me to the airport police station where they filed a report and kept my gun. They wouldn't let us board our flight, so we had to rebook on the next flight to make our event in Green Bay.

We heard nothing about the incident for more than a month. That is until a letter arrived via mail, which explained that I could reclaim my weapon by calling a phone number. But when I called the number, they had no record of the incident or of my weapon. So I called my lawyer to get his advice.

He suggested we contact a defense attorney he recommended. That attorney informed us that he would contact the district attorney's office and ask for the charges to be dropped given my clean record after we paid him a $5,000 retainer. Eventually, the case was dismissed and no charges were filed, on the condition I take a gun safety class and file three letters from character witnesses who were not family members.

But the entire drama took a huge toll on me. I was terrified I might end up in jail. I worried the potential reputational damage would destroy my speaking career. While driving home from the attorney's office, I was on the verge of a nervous breakdown.

When we got home, I called our family doctor and asked him to prescribe something to settle me down. Our family doctor is also a good friend. Over the course of the previous few months, he had asked about my drinking habits: how much I was drinking each day, and if I had cut down. Looking back, I can see how the medications and the alcohol were clouding my thinking. If I had been of clear mind, that gun would have never ended up in my backpack.

"Listen, with all the medications you're taking, you have got to stop drinking," my doctor said when I went to his office to pick up the prescription. "I don't know what Parkinson's does to a body, but I know what you're doing to yours. Do you need help quitting?"

I looked him straight in the eye and said, "I can quit anytime that I want. I just don't want to yet."

He prescribed a seven-day supply of Clonazepam, a tranquilizer used to treat panic disorders. Though the prescription was low dosage, the results were high-octane. Especially when mixed with everything else I was taking.

I don't remember the Christmas of 2016. I don't remember who was around, what I did, or what gifts were exchanged. I don't remember any pictures. They showed me a snapshot and I was in it, but I don't remember it being taken.

We had family at our house that Christmas: our kids and our parents. My daughter Jessica suspected something was wrong with me because I was more detached than usual. It all came to a head on Christmas Eve. Shawna was furious with me and embarrassed because I was being belligerent. I was complaining about my pain, and turning into a mean little drunk. I could tell she was at her wit's end, I just didn't recognize it. It was a crappy existence.

After dinner that evening, I started acting strangely, drawing out my words in long drawls, and slurring terribly. I could hardly walk.

"Something is wrong," I said.

No one was paying attention to how many pills I was taking that Christmas Eve, including me. No one was keeping track of how much vodka and cranberry juice I was drinking. I was a ticking time bomb of anger, pain, alcohol, and medications.

"When did you last eat?" Shawna asked.

"Two. Maybe three, four days ago," I slurred. Truth is, I had no idea when I had last eaten. "Something is really wrong," I repeated.

Shawna thought I might be having a stroke. So Lauren, my daughter-in-law and a hospital chaplain, put me through some tests. She asked me to smile, stick out my tongue, and close my eyes and raise my arms. Apparently, I passed all of these tests. No stroke.

"Babe, I am just so, so tired," I said to Shawna.

Shawna was torn. Should she launch an epic battle and force me to go to the hospital emergency room, or put me to bed? After conferring with Lauren, Shawna decided she best let me sleep off the effects of the medications and alcohol. I nodded off as soon as she put me to bed.

That was when Shawna decided to count the pills in my medicine bottles. She discovered that, over a twenty-four-hour period, I had taken eight pills from a twenty-count Clonazepam prescription. The dosage regimen was one Clonazepam every eight hours. But in my alcohol, drug, and pain-addled haze, I was taking Clonazepam along with—and in the same manner as—Oxycodone: two pills every four hours.

I should've been dead.

While I slept, Shawna and the kids held a meeting. My kids were terrified after witnessing my behavior; I was not acting like the dad they knew and loved. They were barely aware of all of the surgeries I had undergone. We didn't want them to worry. But this behavior was far beyond that of patients recovering from surgery. Shawna now knew that she needed to closely monitor every single pill I took. And every vodka and cranberry juice I mixed. She took my pills and hid them from me and poured out every bottle of alcohol in the house.

Shawna kept tabs on me throughout the night, making sure I was still breathing. The next day, Christmas, I celebrated the birth of Jesus by sleeping off the effects of an overdose. The following morning, Shawna texted our family doctor informing him of what happened on Christmas Eve. He suggested she check me into a rehab facility immediately.

At first, Shawna protested. I had two speaking engagements booked in January and we both hated to cancel these commitments. It's akin to breaking your word.

"You can deal with this now and save his life, or you can wait until it's too late and plan for his funeral," the doctor responded. He recommended a rehab facility and urged her to call immediately.

Before I got out of bed, Shawna was on the phone with The Treatment Center of the Palm Beaches (now The Treatment Center by The Recovery Village) in Lake Worth, Florida. They wanted to admit me that very day. She explained this was a practical impossibility since I was in Texas. They also advised that people generally enter the center alone, another practical impossibility given my condition. So they suggested Shawna escort me to Florida and promised to pick us up at the airport.

She summoned me from our bedroom and sat me in my favorite leather chair. I was still in a horrible mood, angry at the pain racking my body and the grogginess in my head from the overdose. Shawna informed me that she had called our doctor, and he said I had to enter treatment immediately.

"Screw the doctor!" I snapped.

But Shawna and the kids calmly insisted I needed help. I grudgingly agreed.

Shawna pressed me to call the doctor and The Treatment Center while she booked flights along with a hotel reservation for her overnight stay in Florida. The Center charged $1,000 per day for its treatment services, and insurance only covered a small part of the total bill. So, we would have to raid the $35,000 we had been saving to redo our backyard and build a fence.

While the kids were in the house, I managed to keep my composure. But as soon as they left to return home, I let my fear and anger take over. In my pissed-off, afraid-of-the-unknown state, I started cleaning. I purged everything I could get my hands on, filling two large garbage bags with stuff. To this day, I have absolutely no idea what was in those bags.

"What are you doing?" Shawna asked.

"I need clothes," I replied forcefully. "You can come with me or not, but I'm going out to get clothes."

"What?"

"If I'm going to Florida, I need clothes." (Addiction makes you selfish.)

So I went to the store and bought Polo shirts, Polo shorts, workout shorts, and comfortable shoes. I got a face wash that smelled great. Knowing I'd be sharing a room with another strung-out resident, I bought pajama pants. I spent more than $900 on new duds—my way of protesting this sudden and unwelcome junket to rehab. Tragically, none of these new clothes followed me home after my thirty-five-day spell. Everyone at The Center smoked so much that my clothes were saturated with that stale, acrid stench. I just left them there for some other poor soul.

I also bought an iPod, as cell phones were forbidden. Shawna filled it with music: my heavy metal—*Disturbed, AC/DC, Metallica*—to soundtrack my workouts, and

Shawna's Christian worship music—*Jesus Culture, Jeremy Camp, Bethel Music*—to calm me for reflection. A weird, bipolar mix when you think about it.

When we got home from my shopping spree, I started packing. I stuffed a suitcase with all of my new clothes, and as many coloring books, pens, and pencils as I could jam into the remaining pockets and spaces.

At 3:00 a.m., two days after Christmas, we left home to catch a flight from San Antonio International Airport to Dallas-Fort Worth International, where we would make our connection to Ft. Lauderdale, Florida. While sitting in the DFW Skylink train on our way to the terminal to make our Ft. Lauderdale connection, I looked over at Shawna.

"I don't know why I'm doing this," I said. "I'm just trusting you."

Through the good times and the bad, it is *trust* that sustains a marriage. I was in no position to make any decisions. My trust in Shawna helped save my life.

We were met at Fort Lauderdale–Hollywood International Airport by a short man in a black sedan. It was a forty-five-minute ride to The Treatment Center. We got there around noon, and as soon as we got through the door, Shawna started filling out paperwork, listing the medications I had been taking and when my last dosage was. We sat on a white couch in this tiny waiting area behind locked doors. I clung to my suitcase while staring at a picture of the beach in an aluminum frame. But this was no resort.

A few minutes later, we were saying our goodbyes. Shawna left for her hotel room in tears, unsure of what would happen to me—or to us—over the next month. She had a flight back to Texas the next morning. It would be the longest period of time we would be apart over the course of our marriage.

After Shawna left, the Center staff did a complete search of my suitcase. I was immediately escorted by a couple of male counselors to a tiny barren room. They offered me a glass of tea—fake tea with no caffeine. It was awful.

"Strip, Mr. Morris," one of the men said sternly.

I could hardly believe what I was hearing. The lights in this room were so bright I wanted to cover my eyes. Instead of illuminating the room, the glare made everything seem fuzzy.

"Now, Mr. Morris," he said abruptly. "We need you to remove all of your clothes."

Those lights illuminated the dinginess of the room. There was a faint line of dust and dirt where the now off-white linoleum flooring met the walls. One of the counselors extended his hand to me while simultaneously blocking the door. There was no reason for him to block that door.

Twenty years ago, I probably could have taken these bozos out without much effort. I could probably have done it then too, but everything was so fuzzy.

"Mr. Morris? We're waiting."

I begrudgingly stepped out of my shoes and slowly removed my socks, but my balance was off. So, I sat in a chair to begin my pathetic strip tease. I unbuttoned my shirt. The sleeve slid from my left arm to reveal my foot-long tattoo of a cross and the words "Faith, not by sight." It's no coincidence that my tattoo is on my pitching arm, just inches from another foot-long marking—one of the many scars from my dozens of surgeries. I unbuttoned my jeans.

I toughened my resolve and quickly stood, letting my pants and underwear drop to the floor. I stepped out of them. There I was in front of these strangers in all of my fifty-three years of glory, naked as a baby. But the worst was yet to come.

"Mr. Morris, please give us twenty jumping jacks." I did as instructed. *I really wasn't an addict,* I thought to myself as my arms windmilled in the air. *I really didn't need to perform jumping jacks buck naked in front of rehab orderlies to see if smuggled drugs would jiggle out of my rear end.* It was sobering.

Then they had me lean on a chair and bend over for a closer inspection—the exclamation point on my ceremonious initiation into rehab. This was worse than the G-string that said, "Ring my Bell."

After I had jumped all the jacks and had my anal probe, I sat in my room and stared at all the coloring books I had brought with me. *What in the hell is all of this?* Though it was against the rules, I mustered my charm and persuaded a staff member to let me call Shawna. I insisted that my life depended on it.

"I need books," I said.

"Excuse me? You need books?" she said on the other end of the line.

"I need books or I am going to go crazy."

So Shawna took a taxi to the airport, rented a car, drove to a bookstore, and bought me three books by thriller novelist Brad Thor. She delivered them before I went to bed that night. I don't think I ever read them. There wasn't time.

I ate a stack of crackers for dinner and returned to my room where I collapsed onto my bed and stared at the camera installed in the corner of the ceiling—a blatant reminder that I would never be alone in this place.

The next chapter of my life had begun.

❧

I celebrated the coming of the New Year my first week at the center. No fireworks. No parties. No fun. The food was terrible: no seasoning, no spices, no saltshakers. We dined one evening on what was supposedly filet mignon, but I'd swear on a stack of Bibles it was flank steak minus any seasoning. The cook was really proud of it though. I lost fifteen pounds after eating nothing but soup for a week.

The Center was a dump, like a dilapidated nursing home. I called it the last resort for the last resort—and it was...for people like me.

That first week, I didn't sleep well. Our room was pitch black with the door closed—save for the red light on the surveillance camera. But every twenty minutes, a staff member would open the door and come into the room to check on us, flooding it with blinding light from the hallway.

All of the chairs, mattresses, and pillows in the entire facility were covered in plastic to protect them from the vomit and feces expelled from detoxing bodies. Every time one of us moved or shifted our weight to get comfortable, the crunchy noises from the plastic seemed to fill the hallway, adding to the wakefulness.

I was lucky. I didn't experience any of the typical horrors associated with coming off the medications and alcohol: no puking or pooping, no debilitating migraines, chills, fevers, or stroke-like symptoms. My body adapted well to the detox process. Little did I know that my wife and her group prayer ladies were praying specifically for my detox to be mild.

One of my roommates was a teenage alcoholic, the other a man about my age with sleep apnea. But people came and went from the center regularly. I saw several leave the center before they completed the program—the temptation of addiction was simply too much. They abandoned all of their personal belongings and disappeared. Others were making secret calls to their drug dealers, making arrangements to meet them for a score after they got out. Still others didn't make it past the airport bar after they were released. They succumbed in the first few hours. Or they'd get into a fight.

I made one good friend at The Center: Smitty. He had worked for a national security agency before securing a number of high-level positions with Fortune 500 companies. He was on his third round of rehab. He professed to be a Christian. His wife had left him and gained sole custody of his kids. He ended up at The Center after he wrapped his car around a tree and left the scene. The judge gave him a choice: rehab or jail.

He was depressed just before he left The Center to go home, and I told him he was going to have to earn back the trust of his kids if he was truly going to recover. I encouraged him to work at it. A couple of weeks after we had returned home, he called me and shared a Valentine's card his daughter had made for him. He had secured a top-level position with a big company. He disappeared a month after getting that job. I haven't heard from him since, despite my attempts to connect with him. I don't think his family has heard from him either.

To protect the residents from themselves, the staff locked up cologne. They locked up razors too. Sometimes people would go into rooms of other residents, scouring the space for razors to commit suicide. To shave, we'd have to check out our razors, and then check them back in.

I was fuming those first couple of days, pissed off by the annoyances. My roommates smoked like freight trains. In fact, cigarette smoke surrounded the place and it drove me crazy. It brought back memories of my father, who smoked with us in the car, the windows rolled up, even though I suffered from asthma. To relieve my angst, I colored. I checked out. I didn't participate.

That's when my patient advocate Sonja paid me a visit. "Either you get to work, get to your classes, and get healthy, or get out of here," she said firmly. A statuesque African American woman, Sonya was a Type A "get 'er done" type of person. She was a recovering addict herself and she knew what it took to change.

"Look at these people, puking and pooping everywhere," I said, "They're out of control. These people look like they've been through hell."

Sonya looked at me and in the sweetest possible voice said, "You look like that too, honey."

She was right. For the first time in weeks, I looked in the mirror. I barely recognized the unshaved guy with glassy eyes staring back at me. I remembered the words my grandfather used to always tell me, "Don't judge people until you get to know what's on their inside."

It was easy to tell who was in the first week of their stay at the center—they were mad at the world. They didn't care about anything or anyone. After being one of those incredibly pissed-off people, I learned it's best to steer clear of them, at least for a few days.

One of the pastors at The Center absolutely loved baseball. He had been to every ballpark in the country and had stories, pictures, and paraphernalia from each of them in his office. When he found out I was there, he wanted to talk to me.

"What do you think your problem is?" he asked. "Do you think Jesus is not with you?"

"Jesus is always with me," I answered. "He's my copilot."

"If you had Jesus with you, why wouldn't you let him be the pilot?"

"Huh…I never thought of it like that. Why wouldn't I let him be in charge?"

After that conversation, I got it. That was the fifth day. So for the next thirty days, I focused on getting better. It was the first time in my life that I got to concentrate on just me. No excuses—just reality.

I was slowly getting a grip—coming out of my anger phase—when I first met Kemoy, my counselor.

"Nice to meet you," she said, after calling me down to her office. She had been out of town during my first few days at the center.

"I'm ready," I said.

"Say that again?" Kemoy was a striking African American woman, very calm and caring.

"I want to do whatever I have to do to make things right," I said. "I want to get better. What do I need to do?"

"Well then, let's get to work."

My first group therapy session was an eye-opening experience. I listened to others tell their stories. I watched them try to cope without their substance of choice—crack, heroin, alcohol, opioids. I listened to twenty and twenty-five-year-old people complain about how they'd been wronged. "It's my mom's fault," or "It's my boyfriend's fault," or "It's my wife's fault. It's not my fault."

"You're an idiot," the instructor would say. "You know that?" She didn't hesitate to call them out.

Another person was practically in a coma and slept through all the sessions. Yet another person was constantly chewing on candy—his dose of quasi-methadone. It was during these group sessions that I heard, for the first time, people telling stories of their journey to recovery. This works. That doesn't work. This was my rock bottom. This is my third time here. Some of their stories were so far removed from my personal experiences that I started a conversation with myself.

Nope. Never done that.

How is that person even alive?!

No way in the world I'd ever do that.

One guy told of buying a hit of heroin at 3:00 a.m. after he sold his kid's dog.

"Man, these people are addicts," I finally said out loud.

"Jimmy, don't lose your humble," Sonja countered.

When the fog lifted and the synapses in my brain started firing and connecting, I had to face myself, to confess the depths of what I've done.

"I need help. I can't do this by myself." But God.

Life at The Center was class-driven. Monday through Thursday, I attended several classes each day. Alcoholics Anonymous. Narcotics Anonymous. Bible studies that revealed how the sacred stories of scripture connect to the anxieties and pains in life. Art classes. Meditation classes. Physical Activity classes like kickball. And I'm thinking, why am I doing this? This isn't going to teach me to quit drinking or how to stop taking drugs.

At every class we were required to get our personal role sheets stamped to verify attendance. If we didn't get all of our class stamps each day, then that day didn't count in our recovery process. We lived for the stamps.

The most powerful truth I learned in these classes was that I am not alone. As I listened to the successes and failures of those who had battled addiction, I realized the true power of community. I especially realized the power of my faith. I was reminded that even in the midst of our struggles, it is imperative that we look hard and intentionally at our blessings and summon feelings of gratitude.

You begin to see the light in people's eyes after the first week at the center. You get a glimpse of a person full of dreams and hopes and fears as they fight to be free of the fog of addiction. I started a pain management track the second week, exploring different ways of treating my pain—acupuncture, massage, chiropractic therapies, and heat laser treatments.

I tried Tai Chi, but I found it's almost impossible to balance on one leg when you have difficulty balancing on two.

"I see you're having a problem," the instructor said.

"My problem is I have Parkinson's," I replied in frustration.

"We need to formulate a plan for you to be able to do this."

"Are you going to give me a third leg?"

Sometimes I was not the best student.

My first trip away from The Center was for acupuncture treatments. When I got off the van, I freaked out after leaving the safe space and support that The Center provided. I wasn't ready to deal with the freedom of everyday life yet. The treatments didn't do much for me and I discovered I am not a fan of acupuncture.

But massage was always welcome, and adjustments from the chiropractor seemed to help. But nothing compares to heat laser treatment. These therapies use light energy from a laser to reduce pain and inflammation, relax muscles, accelerate the healing of damaged tissues, and stimulate nerve regeneration. They treated my neck and spine, the areas where I've had fusions and where scar tissue is most dense. It felt incredible—simply divine. I've continued with some of these treatments since leaving The Center.

Toward the end of the first week, I started writing Shawna letters. I didn't have access to a computer, so I actually had to write them by hand. In an earlier, simpler time, a handwritten letter was a treasure of sorts. It was tangible manifestation of the investment of time in a relationship. But waiting on handwritten letters during a month-long stay—especially in this era of instant communication—is inefficient. So Sonya would scan my letters into a computer and email them to Shawna.

Hi Babe—

I am really missing you. I hope you are well. Hug Jaimee and Max for me. We had a pretty incredible A.A. speaker today. Jumped out of airplanes on demand. I am learning a lot of things, positive and negative. I am positive I want to be sober and have a great marriage. Negative in that I have no privacy.

Overall, a good experience. Know that I love you and miss you dearly. Thanks for taking care of everything at home.

I love you,

Jimmy

Without a cell phone, tablet, or computer for distractions, I had a lot of time to reflect—to just to sit and think. It was the first time in my life I paid attention to me—to my emotions and to all of my pain. Without drugs or alcohol suppressing everything in a haze, memories started to emerge.

I remembered being in New York for the first time, walking to the bullpen in the old Yankee Stadium—that historic ballpark—and competing against the Yankees. Even though I was thirty-five, I had been assigned rookie duties by veteran ballplayers—stupid stuff for which they later apologized. One of my jobs in the bullpen was to carry a candy bag, which is easily mistaken for a ball bag. I didn't pitch that game, so my time in the bullpen was spent taking in all the sights and sounds: the fans, the ballpark, the inter-actions on the field.

After the game, I grabbed the candy bag and was heading out when heard this deep, deep voice yell, "Hey! Morris!"

I turned around and spotted a huge cop looking my direction. "Hey! Morris! I gotta question for you," he shouted.

Of course, I knew his question. He wanted a baseball. Everyone who goes to a game wants a baseball. And having an actual player toss you a baseball is one of the most memo-rable experiences at the ballpark.

"Man, I would love to give you a baseball," I said, "but this is just a bag of candy. If you want some candy, I can toss you a couple pieces."

"I need you to sign a ball for me," the cop replied.

He opened a few of his buttons on his uniform and pulled out a baseball. Only in New York does a cop come to the ballpark carrying his own baseball. He tossed it down to me and, as I'm signing it, he says, "Man, that's such a cool story." I smiled.

We were in New York for four days, and for three of those days I firmly planted myself in left field during batting practice and warm-ups. I wanted nothing to do with the bleacher creatures in right field. New York fans are brutal. They're fiercely loyal to their home team and their ritual chants are a storied part of Yankee lore. If you didn't play for the pinstriped team, the bleacher creatures mercilessly harassed you, and every other opposing player.

On the fourth day, the Rays right-hander Roberto Hernandez, my best friend on the team who I called Bert, escorted me across the outfield.

"Come on, rookie, you gotta get it over with," he demanded.

As soon as I was within earshot of the creatures, they started yelling.

"Morris! Hey Morris!"

At first, I tried to ignore them, but they shouted all the louder.

"Morris! We're talking to you, Morris!"

"They are going to keep yelling until you turn around," Bert said.

I took a deep breath and turned around, now staring straight into the countless eyes of the rowdy bleacher creatures.

"You suck!"

I shook my head. *Great, here it comes.*

"It's a great story, but you suck anyway."

And that was it.

I turned back around and tried to hide my smile. I guess the bleacher creatures actually do have a heart after all.

Bert just stared at me. "That's not fair," he said, "it's supposed to be way worse than that." It's strange how memories crop up when you least expect them.

I made some really dumb decisions after retiring from the Major Leagues. The doctors prescribed pills. I prescribed vodka. Over that span of time, I lost sight of who I was. I rested on past successes and forgot about my dreams.

The Rookie happened, but that's not all of who I am; that's just something I did. The cool side of *The Rookie* was the promise I made to those high school kids. That turned into something huge and life-changing. The other side of the story is I was dealing with major life struggles—growing up with a dad who was a terror, enduring physical pain, and supporting a family with a fraying marriage. When I read my Bible, when I prayed, and when I meditated, I had to work through those memories. The Center gave me time and permission to do this away from center stage, away from the next surgery, away from everyone.

The Center gave me hope there was a different way to live, that there are still new chapters in my story that need to be lived and written. It gave me permission to listen to my heart and start dreaming new dreams.

Many people remember that classic 1980's anti-drug commercial by the Partnership for a Drug-Free America featuring an egg. "This is your brain," says the narrator holding up an egg. "This is drugs," he says motioning to a frying pan. He cracks the egg and fries the contents. "This is your brain on drugs. Any questions?"

According to Dr. Manuel Montes, a psychiatry specialist at The Center, addiction occurs when other substances hijack the reward system of the brain. Dopamine is a neurotransmitter, a chemical that is responsible for helping the nerve cells in the brain transmit signals. Dopamine levels affect our emotions, our movements, and our sensations of pleasure and pain. Low dopamine levels in specific areas of the brain is among the key indicators of Parkinson's disease. And since Parkinson's is a disease attributed to a lack of dopamine, it is commonly treated with dopaminergic drugs and opioids.

My diagnosis of CTE-induced Parkinson's and peripheral neuropathy, and the resultant pain throughout my body, was treated with multiple opioids. It was a perfect storm for addiction, without motivating any behavioral changes.

The ventral tegmental area (VTA) is the brain's reward center. Whenever a person achieves something rewarding, the VTA releases dopamine to the *nucleus accumbens*. They feel a sense of accomplishment, which is interpreted as "pleasure." This feeling reinforces whatever behavior you just conducted. Do something right, feel good. Repeat. It's a fairly simple formula. The more dopamine that is released into the brain, the more satisfaction you will feel. Behaviors that stimulate the release of dopamine are then stored as memories. The more dopamine released, the more important the memory.

Drugs, like painkillers, simulate and hijack the dopamine reward system. Addiction happens when memories, the part that motivates behaviors, have been compromised.

According to evolutionary biology, the most important activity for humans is reproduction. That is why an orgasm releases the highest natural level of dopamine possible: it's the reward for procreative activities. But the synthetic chemicals we can now introduce into our brains offer four to eight times the dopamine hit produced by an orgasm. Once that massive level of dopamine reaches the nucleus accumbens, it's stored in the brain as a memory with the highest priority.

This is now the ultimate pleasure. This is now what the body wants more than anything. These drugs change the structure and function of the brain at the expense of rewarding previous normal behaviors. When an addicted person does something that releases normal levels of dopamine, they no longer feel the same sense of pleasure—they lose the internal motivation to continue performing normal activities. The drugs have successfully co-opted the neurotransmitter system. And this phenomenon is not completely voluntary.

If addiction were treated by radically altering the physical structure of the brain, destroying the nucleus accumbens for example, that person would no longer derive pleasure from *anything*—sex, food, or a good movie. They would end up permanently depressed and less than human.

That's why, when a person is denied the drugs they are addicted to, what follows is a natural state of depression. According to Dr. Montes, the saying "once an addict, always an addict" is true. The changes are, for all practical purposes, irreversible and permanent. It is impossible to go back to how things were previously. For those who have experienced addiction in any form, they now have to learn to live with a new normal. Education about the destructive power of drugs truly is the best prevention.

Recovering from addiction is just like recovering from a severe injury that requires surgery to heal. Surgery affects the entirety of the body. I have to go to rehab and train to get back to where I was. I have to make adjustments to the changes that were made in my body. I have to learn to live with it.

The medications doctors often prescribe have led to an epidemic of opioid abuse. When addicts can't get their highs from legal prescriptions, they turn to heroin, street fentanyl, or worse. Statistically speaking, though only 1 percent of the population struggles with addiction, it costs our society close to $70 billion annually in lost productivity, family breakdown, legal and medical expenses, law enforcement, and treatment.

The good news is that if a person can stay clean and sober for ninety days, brain function can begin to recover and heal to the extent possible. Unfortunately, if you have insurance that will pay, it only pays for thirty days. And the depression levels an addict feels while trying to detox is at its worst at the end of thirty days. That explains why relapses are so common.

Listening to Dr. Montes spell out the differences between normal brains and addicted brains—and what it means to be human—was a profound educational experience for me.

Hi Babe—

Thank you and Chelsey for writing. And thank you for more clothes. By the time I talk to you, I should have them. First off, I understand you being scared and apprehensive about when I come home. Any words or promises are going to fall on deaf ears—I get that. Let me just say I know my behavior is what counts. One day at a time I will rebuild my ability to be trusted by you. Here is what I know.

Painkillers cause pain and they kill you. I will never ask a doctor again about my pain. Now that my mind is clear and I have talked to a multitude of doctors and psychiatrists multiple times a week, I understand something: I have been mad at Parkinson's, not my dad (forgiven). I have been furious at the disease itself. The only way this disease can kill me is if I help it. I am no longer willing to do that. I was crying out for help because I didn't want you or the kids to perceive my weakness. Again thank you. I will take the pain and clearness over ever altering my mind.

For me, some very important revelations have occurred.

God gets to lead, never take that for granted.

The only way I do not help this disease is God.

I know for a fact He will take my pain and make it a gain for someone.

My love and respect for you.

Humbled, humiliated—He got my attention. This will be used in the future as God sees fit.

Again, I know my words are empty, my behavior I will let speak for itself. I love you with all my heart. The anger is gone—if I have anger in my heart there is no room for God to work. I have even learned meditation. My next goal is yoga. Will never be able to bounce and jump around, but yoga can help. Have

Tai Chi coming up also. Want to check that out too.

My physical issues of not being able to do what I have always done to get in shape almost destroyed me. I have to roll with the punches and do what makes me stronger and I couldn't have a better partner than you to go through this next stage of life with.

Even though I will have 10 days left, I graduate next Thursday. Not exactly what I wanted to graduate from, but God has a way of getting our attention. I still have classes to the end of the month. No still time.

Babe, I love you and do not want to ever jeopardize that.

I love you,
Jimmy

P.S. They are giving me lots of tools and horror stories to load in my toolbox. Coming home loaded, in a different way. Love you!

∞

My third week at the center was marked by the perpetual presence of Kleenex. This is the time when you cry because your roommate's kid got a job, or you saw a TV commercial featuring a devoted dog, or you experienced one bite of food that tasted really good. The third week is when all of those emotions that have been shoved far down finally start to emerge.

Good stories teach us how to feel what other people are feeling, and that time was a complete roller coaster of emotions. I'd be visiting with someone and be perfectly fine and then suddenly would be rendered speechless and completely caught off guard by the power of the sentiments rising within.

Of course, I know there's no crying in baseball. But this wasn't baseball, this was life.

But there were times I cried because I was thankful for the opportunity to play the game. I cried because I missed my home, my family, and my amazing wife. I cried because I realized I had been given a second chance to tell others how my story is a part of God's story.

Don't lose your humble. I know I'm far from perfect in this area, but I'm learning. God does not give up on anyone. Humility is remembering that I'm an "anyone." It was also during this emotional period that I finally learned to stop feeling sorry for myself. Even during my most intense struggles, when I stopped to think intentionally about my blessings, I noticed a significant attitudinal shift.

I was learning to keep my humble. I was also reminded of how much I enjoyed movement. I was an athlete after all, and I missed the physicality. I started walking.

Parkinson's wants to stop those it afflicts from moving. When you stop moving, the disease progresses and the pain intensifies. At the center, I fought it by walking.

I would get up at 4:30 a.m.—while it was still dark— and start walking the short loop, lined with palm trees, around the premises before the smokers took over. Walking helped me reset. I did this instead of coloring. I discovered that my coloring habit was about pushing people away and retreating into solitude. I was done with that crap.

So I gave all of my coloring books and pens to a girl from group therapy that was getting ready to be discharged. She suffered from bipolar disorder, which probably spurred her efforts to self-medicate, driving her to addiction. During her first two weeks at the center, she was a nightmare. She had screaming fits and dramatic mood swings. She was either exuberantly happy or crying her brains out. At one point, she tried to leave the premises and set off the building's alarms.

I told her to focus on keeping within the lines to take her mind off drugs. In the last two weeks she was there, she was really serious about recovery. I like to think my coloring books buoyed that process.

In the first few days of my new routine I couldn't quite walk a mile, which was seventeen-and-a-half laps. But by the end of my third week, I was walking 102 laps a morning—between five and six miles. All of this walking was supervised—I had grown used to constantly being surveilled.

"What do you do to escape the walls?" Kemoy asked me during a group therapy session,

"When I walk, in my mind, I can walk anywhere in the world I want to," I responded. "I can walk through Rome or Switzerland, or Hawaii and Jamaica."

I think God gave us imaginations not only to help us dream big dreams, but also to help keep us sane. My imagination helped me wall off some of the horrible experiences I'd had growing up with my father. It also helped me remember there was a great big world beyond this center, and this experience would help me make the most of my time in that world once I'm better.

As long as I can keep moving, there is hope.

The fourth week at the center marked the return of grooming and self-care. You sit up straighter in classes. You wear cologne to chapel and church services. You care about how you look and are quick to judge the appearances of others.

Don't lose your humble, Morris.

During this week, I started thinking long and hard about new dreams I wanted to chase, and which dreams mattered most to me. I wanted to keep telling my story, to bring hope and help across the country. I wanted to use my foundation to help other kids find hope and a sense of achievement through sports. I wanted to have a great marriage with Shawna, and to be a good dad as my kids went out into the world.

Without a new dream to chase, without new stories to create and new adventures to live, it's tempting to just coast through life.

I learned a lot in my thirty-five days at The Treatment Center. I saw people at their worst clinging to hope and to the possibility of a different way of living. I began my stay as one of those sarcastic, cynical souls who didn't fully appreciate the horrors I was introducing into my body—until I saw the effects in others. Sonya and Kemoy and all the staffers at the center give of their lives—not for a six-figure paycheck or dreams of a Disney movie—but to help people get started down the right path. I know I will be mulling over those lessons for years to come.

I was ready to start living a new normal: no more drinking and no more embarrassing trips to the convenience store, no more pain pills and no more clumsy, disastrous overdoses.

In reality, each day brings a new normal. When I wake up, I don't know what parts of my body will hurt and what parts will be pain free. I don't know how my body will respond to whatever tasks I have in front of me. I have to accept the challenges and move on.

In the movie *The Book of Eli*, starring Denzel Washington, the character Eli hears a message from God, which in turn becomes his mission. He encounters daily pushback and life-threatening moments but he keeps going, determined to fulfill his purpose. I know I still have a purpose.

Change is difficult for all of us. But learning how to lean into changes and discover the good in them is where I have trained my focus.

I've always been a person on the move—quick to go. I can't always live that way now with my physical challenges. I have to intentionally slow things down, probably not a bad idea at this stage of my life. I have to intentionally think about providing my body adequate rest while, at the same time, pushing it beyond what's comfortable. When you're young, you think you're invincible. You take big risks and expect your body to respond. But those risks come at a cost.

I learned about the need for tolerance, how to suspend judgment, and the importance of listening to other people's stories. People from every background you can possibly imagine suffer from addiction. Their behaviors are often the result of pain, tragedy, and bad choices. The Bible says that we shouldn't judge others. That is The Lord's job. Jesus never turned away from anyone. But I believe he will leave them to their choices. After all, we do have free will.

The conversations you have with yourself are powerful. For too many years my dad's words echoed in my mind. Eventually, I learned to silence those words, only to have a diagnosis of Parkinson's and peripheral neuropathy open new floodgates of negative self-talk.

This is too hard.
I can't do this.
Throw in the towel.

This affliction is beyond my control, but with Christ I can do anything! Not losing my humble means not trying to control everything. But keeping my humble also means remembering I'm not alone on this journey. I don't have to alienate my friends and family as I discover and navigate my new normal.

Now that all the drugs are out of my system, I feel a profound shift in my life. I am much more aware of the breadth and depth of my emotions, feelings I have ignored and repressed for far too long. Acknowledging them leads to a fuller, more rewarding life.

That's why I must have hope—hope in the power of truth, hope that as I continue to travel and share my story, those who suffer from addiction, Parkinson's, and other afflictions will also find hope and strength for their journeys.

I have hope that those who are addicted to opioids might find the answers they are looking for and the courage to take a step toward health and healing. I have hope for the students and communities I get to work with through my foundation. Sports can be an incredible tool for life change. Most importantly, I have hope that in my marriage and in my relationships with my kids that some of our best days are still ahead us.

Parts of this new normal are incredibly frustrating. But if I choose to live in the past, to dwell on those things I can no longer do or change, I can easily lose sight of the work God has for me now. I am incredibly grateful for the opportunities I've been given as a result of my stint in the Majors and the success of *The Rookie*. I know God will be with me as I plumb new adventures and inscribe more chapters in my life.

❦

The day I graduated from The Treatment Center with a degree I didn't really want, I was asked to say a few words to the residents. I was a little rusty. It had been close to two months since my last speaking engagement. I figured this crowd didn't want to hear my usual story. So I talked about what brought me to the center and my observations during my stay. I began with opioids.

"Opioids make you crave sugar, and I had been eating a lot of sugar back home. Alcohol is also pure sugar. So when I put on my jeans for the first time in a month, they fell off. You may gripe and complain about the food here, but I know it's better than stale Doritos and hot beer."

There were a few chuckles, so I continued.

"And what is it with the plastic covering the mattresses and the pillows? How is anyone supposed to get a good night's rest with all the noise being made each and every time we move in our beds? Maybe, just maybe, if our bodies didn't poop and puke all over ourselves and everywhere trying to get these drugs out of our systems, we could get rid of the plastic?"

Now, everyone was laughing.

"There's not a day that goes by where someone isn't whining or complaining about not being permitted to use their cell phone. 'Why can't I use my cell phone? I'm an adult!'

"Friends, really? Be completely honest with yourselves and with me. Because if you had access to your cell phone, we all know you would find some way, somehow, to get drugs delivered to you while you're here.

"If you look around the edges of this room, some of these staffers you may like, some of them you may not like, and some of them you might even say you hate. But these staffers are angels—each and every one of them. They aren't doing this work to get rich or become famous. They are here because they know what you're going through and they want to see you to the other side. They want to help you be the best you possible. They know the struggles, they know the pain, they know that some will be coming back here again. Still, they choose hope. And that's powerful."

At this point, there weren't many dry eyes in the room. I'd only been talking for about three minutes, by far the shortest speech I'd ever given. One of the staffers asked if I could keep talking.

"I think I'm good. Thanks for all you've done," I responded.

On the day I left The Treatment Center of the West Palm Beaches, I looked back and noted everything I didn't see the very first time I came to the building. I saw the place where I got my life back. It was run down and tattered, kind of like me. The Treatment Center is a hard place. But good things can come through hard places. It made me respect what I have and who I am.

Life may be hard, and life may not be fair, but that doesn't mean life isn't good.

Being back at home was scary at first. It had been a long time since I had not been under the influence of something. It was like relearning body parts after a prolonged surgery. Is this room still the same? Is the bathroom the same? Does my dog still love me?

There is so much we take for granted. We don't realize how quickly it can change and be taken away. At the center, I learned so much more outside of class than in the classroom—just by watching people. I observed their behaviors, and I could tell who would be most likely to fall off the wagon. These poor souls just couldn't quit talking about how good they felt when they were high. And I thought, *How do you know? You were high.*

Four days after leaving The Treatment Center, I had my first speaking event. I was escorted to a green room behind the stage with an open liquor cabinet displaying every kind of spirit imaginable—all for free.

"Help yourself!" they said.

"No thanks. Do you have Dr. Pepper?"

It wasn't even that hard to say no. I know quite well what that will do to me. I have learned and remembered who I am. And I have no desire to return to The Treatment Center. Ever.

That first speech out of recovery was a little rough. I was off, and I couldn't find a rhythm. I was slotted as the last speaker of the event and scheduled for early in the morning. After a full slate of activities from the prior day and a long night, everyone was ready to go home. It was probably a good start, as rough as it was.

Just a couple days afterwards, I had my second speaking engagement. This one was perfect. I felt God's tangible presence in the silence of the crowd as I spoke. I received a standing ovation at the conclusion. It was an incredibly affirming and encouraging experience.

I learned that if I worked out really hard, my brain had a hard time deciphering between soreness and Parkinson's pain. So I push myself a little harder every day to feel alive and feel like I have a little control over the pain.

At home, I made a friend, Vern, who walked just as much as I did. He was a war veteran who was injured protecting our country. He had knee replacements. One day, I asked how he dealt with the pain.

"Every day I wake up in pain, I know I'm alive," he replied.

So now, every day when I wake up in pain, I know I'm alive and God still has a plan for me.

CHAPTER 10

POWERED BY FAITH

I've had more than a few brushes with death over my more than five decades on this earth, some closer than others. Much closer. One example of the latter happened in 1986 when I was twenty-one years old. I was dating a twenty-eight-year-old nurse from Dallas. Her parents lived in Brownwood, and while on a visit to see them, she came into my grandfather's clothing store. This was after he had passed away, and my father and uncle were running Ernest Morris Menswear (they eventually ran it into the ground).

I was impressed with her, so I asked her out on a date. Not long after, I made the trip from Brownwood to Dallas to pay her a visit. It was in the middle of winter.

After my visit, I scrambled to get back to Brownwood to pack up clothes and equipment and head to Arizona for Spring Training. The roads in Dallas were icy. As I was driving on Lyndon B. Johnson Freeway (I-635), the partial loop around Dallas, to connect with I-35 to head south, I came upon a small upslope. As I crested the incline, I saw a car stopped in my lane with a guy next to it frantically waving his hands. He was warning oncoming traffic of a wreck just ahead.

Hurling toward him in my red five-speed Toyota Celica GT, I stupidly slammed on the brakes in an attempt to stop. My brakes locked and I lost control, spinning on the ice. I twisted across three lanes until I plowed into a barrier on the side of the freeway. I bounced off that barrier and boomeranged back onto the freeway right into the path of an oncoming eighteen-wheeler. The driver slammed on his brakes. I could hear the hiss of the air brakes and the intermittent screech of tires as they scraped over small patches of ice-free pavement.

His bumper was closing in on the driver's side of my car. I watched his front grill grow bigger and bigger in my side window. Time slowed down. I cried out to the Lord in desperation. In my terrorized stupor, I braced for impact. I thought I was dead. *There's no way he can stop on that ice.*

Then, just a couple of feet from my side door, the truck somehow came to an abrupt halt. That grill filled the whole side window of my car—a giant toothy mouth waiting to take a bite out of steel, glass, and flesh. My car was banged up pretty badly. I got a new one out of it. But how did that spin not cut me in half?

Fast forward to December of 2018. We were in Florida for my last two speeches of the year. Only problem was, I had no voice. Due to a digestive issue, I was having problems with bile and acid reflux that was ulcerating my esophagus. The fumes and fluids from the reflux were wreaking havoc with my vocal cords. I could barely muster a whisper.

Still, I refused to cancel these engagements. The sponsors of my talk were in a panic, freaking out in fact. We soothed the situation by telling them that I had a sinus infection from allergies and that everything was going to be fine. I would be able to deliver my talks without a hitch. And I did, though I have no idea how. I stepped out in faith and delivered those speeches to standing ovations. After I spoke and we made our way to the airport to return home, I couldn't talk. My voice was reduced to a shallow whisper. How does that happen? How do you explain it? Are these miracles?

For the first fifteen years of my life, I had no idea what faith was. Sure, I had been to church and my parents made gestures toward faithfulness, but it wasn't really a way of life. There was no depth to it. In fact, I remember a lot of times as a kid going with my family to church on Sunday morning. If the doors to the church were closed when we arrived, we would just drive by and go out to eat breakfast somewhere. It was a convenient excuse not to go in.

At fifteen, after moving from Hollywood, Florida to Brownwood, Texas, I became very familiar with the true meaning of faith, even though I didn't realize it at the time. My grandparents instilled the seeds of faith within me, just by how they lived their lives. Sure, they went to church and Sunday school, sang in the choir, and participated in whatever was going on at Central Methodist Church during the week. My grandfather was a church deacon, my grandmother the church secretary.

But this was in many ways separate from their faith. That, they lived out in their daily lives. They showed grace, forgiveness, and love. They didn't judge people or condescend to them. They were biblical without being religious. They expressed wisdom without being haughty. They strived to live right and do right. And they didn't complain or blame others for their troubles.

"It's our life, and God's in charge," they would always say when confronted with challenges.

From the ages of fifteen to eighteen, I learned that there was a difference between religion and faith. Religion and faith are like oil and vinegar. They don't go together unless you shake them. Vigorously. For me religion is about manmade rules, an invisible yardstick that no one can measure up to. But faith is about extending grace. There is no condemnation or condescension in grace. Those years in Brownwood are when I learned these important distinctions.

I believe faith is very personal. For twenty years I have shared my story and my convictions with groups of people from private businesses, universities, schools, churches and other organizations. I never venture to tell anyone what they should or shouldn't do.

Instead, I relay my lived experiences, beliefs, unexplained events, and what has and hasn't worked for me. It's my story, just like your experiences make up your story. In every speech, I attempt to teach others how to surround themselves with the very best people, how to persevere, how to nurture humility, and how to approach life with a sense of humor. That is how faith has worked in my life.

☙❦❧

On the night of July 26, 2018, I was awakened by mysterious scratching noises on the standing seam metal roof of our Kerrville home. It was 3:11 a.m. The sounds shook our black lab Max awake. Even Shawna, who can sleep through anything, was roused. The sound didn't bother her much though, and she fell back asleep.

But it bothered me. It bothered Max, too. He growled and I noticed the hair on the back of his neck standing at attention. Could it be a raccoon? No, a raccoon wouldn't be able to scurry across the roof's steeply inclined, slick surface. I grabbed my pistol and went looking for the source of the noise. Trained for bird hunting, Max actually hates guns and usually goes in the opposite direction when one is brandished. Not this time. As I made my way around the house, Max was guarding me—from behind, my brave warrior hound. We found nothing.

Max and I returned to the bedroom. I put away my gun, went back to bed, and quickly fell asleep. A few minutes later, I was roused by the sound of Max's growls. I heard that scratching sound again—like talons across the roof. Again, I jumped out of bed and grabbed my gun and, with Max watching my six, headed outside. Again, we found nothing out of the ordinary. We went back to bed and slept through the night, undisturbed.

The following afternoon, I was in the garage lifting weights while Shawna napped inside the house. It was hot. I had both garage doors open for air circulation. Between weightlifting sets, I sat down to rest in a lawn chair facing the weights and a Bose speaker, which was blasting music. *MercyMe* was on tap. I closed my eyes for a few moments and listened to Bart Millard sing "The Hurt and the Healer."

Suddenly I heard voices, strangely vaporous voices. "You are healed, you are healed," they said, over and over. This chorus continued for a few moments before dissipating into a single voice.

"You are healed," it said, in the warmest soothing tone I have ever heard.

I jumped up from my seat, a normally impossible maneuver on account of my Parkinson's. I looked around. *Someone is messing with me*, I thought.

I scanned my surroundings. No one was there. But there was something. Beautiful silver feathers carpeted the ground, hundreds of them. I immediately had this feeling of calm throughout my whole body.

I went into the house to wake Shawna and tell her what had just happened. As I went through the kitchen, I took note of the time on the microwave's digital readout: 3:11 p.m., exactly twelve hours after the scratching noises woke me up the night before.

Coincidence? Who knows? As I walked through the kitchen, I grabbed my DBS (deep brain stimulator) remote. I had been slowly turning it down for months, and with each incremental dip, I felt better. From a high of 4.5, it was now down to 1. For some reason, I was moved to turn it completely off. Not down to .8 or .6, but off.

I felt great. No pain, no loss of balance, no tremors, nothing. With joyful circumspection, I woke Shawna and told her I had turned off my DBS.

"You what?!" she shouted.

Then I did something I had not been able to do for years. I closed my eyes and turned around in a complete circle without falling over or crashing down. I had perfect balance. This may seem like small potatoes to some, but to me it was a big deal. I was cautiously exhilarated.

Shawna was thrilled but stunned. I told her about the voices and what I had seen outside. She hugged me, laughing through tears, and said she wanted to see the feathers. We walked outside. The garage doors were still open. The music was still blaring from the Bose. But there were no feathers, save for a single one.

I know this sounds like *One Flew Over the Cuckoo's Nest*-type stuff, but I saw something. Was it real? Or was it a vision? Biblically, feathers indicate the presence of angels, especially when you find a feather in an odd place.

Crazy? Perhaps. After all, there are birds all over the Texas Hill Country where we lived. But I had never seen that many feathers scattered over a lawn like that. It was like they had come off of the roof. And when you consider they came at that particular moment, what could that possibly mean?

Although the feathers were mostly gone, I knew that God had allowed me to see them. I believe the feathers were a visual promise of his protection through all of our tribulations, safety under his wings. He was with me. With us.

Not long after this strange incident, we got a phone call from the neurologist who programmed my DBS unit. She said that my original DaTSCAN from 2013 showed normal levels of dopamine in my brain—no sign of Parkinson's.

"That's impossible," I said. "We were told I had low dopamine."

That diagnosis had led to the electrode implants in my brain. They had sent the test to a renowned neurologist in Houston who diagnosed my condition as CTE-induced Parkinson's. I exhibited all of the symptoms.

Now, we were being told that my original 2013 diagnosis was wrong. What doctor would offer a specific diagnosis, or rush ahead with risky DBS surgery based on negative test results? The only other explanation is that my original test results were retroactively changed. How plausible is that? A subsequent DaTSCAN confirmed what doctors were now telling us my 2013 tests showed.

Two weeks after I shut down my DBS unit, we paid a visit to my neurologist, Dr. Maria Vikki Alvarez in San Antonio. She examined me, made me walk down the hall, bend over to touch my toes, lean backwards—the whole gamut. I could perform these simple tasks without incident. She couldn't believe her eyes.

"This just doesn't happen," she insisted. "People with Parkinson's do not get better. But somehow you have. I have no explanation."

I smiled at her and told her I believed God had healed me. She smiled too. She didn't disagree. We discussed making arrangements to have the DBS unit removed from my brain and chest. That was the best doctor's appointment we had had in a long time.

God has done incredible things in my life to get my attention. But this was over the top. This was radical. We often miss the miracles that happen to us in our daily lives. But God was clobbering me over the head with these. There is no question that I am healed. The healing process is by no means complete, but I believe that God heals both immediately and gradually over time. And I get stronger, and suffer less, with each passing day.

Do I question my faith? Do I have doubts? Absolutely! I am human and skeptical by nature. As a Christian and a man schooled in science, I can see where the two canons collide at times. But they also enhance one another.

I have been asked numerous times how it is possible that a person who throws 88 miles per hour at the age of twenty can suddenly throw 98 miles per hour pitches at thirty-five—with 85 percent of the deltoid muscle removed from the shoulder. The secular answer is that I worked out hard, got in shape with my high school baseball team, and gained velocity through a rigorous conditioning regimen. The reality is that I was old and fat, and my shoulder precluded me from ever attempting to make a comeback on the pitcher's mound.

In the same vein, God has taken a classic introvert and man of precious few words and turned him into a public speaker, an unwilling one at that, at least at first. I've spoken all over the world to tell a story, not about baseball, but about life. Baseball just happened to be my dream. God used that dream to get my attention and push me forward. When I follow where I am led, everything works out. Faith!

Doctors never understood my outside-the-bell-curve ailments. Surgery seemed to fix things most of the time. Still, we wonder why? Why so much suffering and why so often? Shawna and I have endured many long and agonizing months of ill health. Through it all we've questioned whether God really was good, if we really were fulfilling some God-given purpose. And, if we were truly working his will, why were we afflicted with all of this sickness and pain?

Why maintain a rigorous travel schedule year-round? Why not give up?

The answer: because we believe we were given this platform to inspire, encourage, and motivate others to reach their full potential. We not only believe *in* God, we *believe* God.

Our faith is ours, and ours alone. It has sustained us through all of life's relentless ups and downs, through travel, family crises, marital struggles, doctor appointments, and surgeries and related complications. It's been so difficult that, at times, we didn't know if we could make it through to the other side. We've wept in each other's arms, sobbed alone in the closet, screamed into pillows, shrieked in the car with music blaring, and cried through phone calls with friends and family. Then we realized God has given us these people to lean on and to remind us we are not alone, to pray for us and carry us when we felt we couldn't take another step.

We've traveled to events when I was just days—sometimes hours—out of surgery. This sounds reckless, but when I sign a contract and make a promise, I'm loath to break it (my grandfather still whispers in my ear). God's grace has sustained us and his message has been delivered, not by shoving faith down the throats of listeners, but by sharing our story. I believe God gave us this platform to help others through difficult times, to offer hope and inspire people to persevere when times get so hard you can't see how you can possibly take another step. But God!

If you know your purpose, keep at it. If you don't know it yet, ask God. He will tell you. He will show you. If you can't hear him, get quiet. Be still. Let go of preconceived notions that He is angry and unreachable, too big to notice you. Talk to him like a friend.

"Are you saying God speaks to you?" people often ask.

"Absolutely!" we answer.

"Is it an audible voice?" (In other words, are you crazy?)

"No, it's a word in our hearts, a thought not our own that feels right and true; it's an unexplained event in our lives that leaves us speechless."

What we've experienced through our faith is that the impossible is possible, that God is good, and is always with us.

CHAPTER 11

ON STAGE

I'm probably the unlikeliest person ever to become a public speaker. As a committed introvert, I was never really comfortable getting on the stage and speaking before a crowd. My comfort comes from knowing that I'm saying something that people need to hear. My presentation has evolved over the years to reflect the shifts (dramatic, as of late) in society: what I see going right, and what I see going off the rails.

Everyone has someone in their lives like my grandparents in their formative years, mentors and loved ones who have inspired them. And everyone has a destructive presence in their lives like my father; whether it is someone in their own house, an uncle, or someone down the road like a teacher, a coach, a professor, or a professional colleague.

Ironically, I'm more comfortable in front of large crowds of say 5,000 than I am in front of small gatherings. The bigger the crowd, the more I like it. John Deacon, the introverted and painfully shy bassist from the British rock group Queen, was said to be perfectly comfortable playing and strutting before crowds of 20,000, happy to surrender most of the limelight to flamboyant front man Freddie Mercury. But when approached by small crowds asking for autographs, he would cover his face with his hands in embarrassment and recoil into the background. I can relate.

I remember, once, speaking before a group of ten employees from a company with offices on the thirtieth floor of a high-rise building in Chicago. They were sitting at their desks with their chairs turned around to face me. The company wanted me to motivate them, pep-up the office culture a bit.

They paid me a lot of money to tell these ten people that anything was possible—that they could do better. It was awkward. Standing in an office before ten people is intimidating. If you lose the attention of just one person in a small group, everyone knows it. It was bizarre. But I got through it. They liked it.

Before our recent move to San Antonio, Shawna and I would spend a good chunk of our lives making the sixty-three-mile trek to and from our Hill Country home in Kerrville to San Antonio International Airport. Frequent travel loses its allure quickly.

In fact, airports and airplanes are the most difficult part of being a motivational speaker. Airport bathrooms always have a distinctive odor from the passage of processed food. Terminals always seem to have the pervading aroma of feet. Gas passing is a common occurrence on planes, whether it's due to indigestion from airport cuisine or the change in pressure. It's very funny at times—once you get beyond the fragrance.

Over the last eighteen-plus years I've spent running my motivational speaking company "Three Strikes, You Are

Out," I've given more than 800 speeches throughout the world. You'd think I'd be tired of telling people about my journey from high school baseball coach to one of the oldest rookies ever to play Major League Baseball. Most have already read my story or seen *The Rookie*. But I love telling and retelling that tale—even if it is all about me. My story motivates everyone who hears it, no matter if they love the game or not. It is a classic Horatio Alger tale that not only lets you root for the underdog, it also reminds us that miracles can happen to anyone.

I never know what I'll experience once I reach my destination. Each venue is different and comes with its own set of challenges. Shawna and I once stayed at a tropical resort shortly after it had been ravaged by a hurricane. Alongside professional business travelers were weary refugees and pets. They had actually opened a school in the resort facility for children, and several relief agencies were working to help these people return to normal lives.

We were there to speak and to entertain, and these people were there because their entire lives and been washed away by a violent natural disaster. It was a humbling and powerful reminder of the wisdom of withholding judgment.

Sometimes I just have to laugh at myself when I think of this absurd and astonishing journey I'm undertaking. Like the time I forgot to pack my dress socks for a speaking engagement. I ended up wearing white tube socks. I know ballplayers who think tall socks are cool and always in fashion. Tube socks, however, simply don't belong on stage. Ever.

Or the time my dress shirt was laundered instead of dry-cleaned and arrived washed and pressed—two sizes too small. I couldn't button the top button for fear of choking off my oxygen supply. There's nothing like a tight shirt to impress the ladies and show off a muscular physique or enhance your rooster neck.

Or the time during a black-tie affair I sat next to legendary University of North Carolina basketball coach Dean Smith. I had forgotten my cuff links. So, I fashioned makeshift cuff links out of paper clips and wore them for the evening. MacGyver, the resourceful secret agent character from the 1980s TV series, has got nothing on me.

In one instance, early in my speaking career, after Shawna dropped me off at the airport very early one Sunday morning, I was turned away at the gate when I tried to board my flight. The gate attendants kept telling me I had already boarded.

"How can I have already boarded the plane when I'm standing right here talking to you?" I asked in frustration.

The flight attendants on board approached the man in my seat and asked him to disembark. I would have been ticked off if that had happened to me, but that's when the fun started.

"I'm Jim Morris," I said to the man.

"No, *I'm* Jim Morris," he replied.

"I'm supposed to be going to Palm Springs."

"No, I'm supposed to be going to Palm Springs."

"I'm going to speak at an event there."

"No, I am."

At the time, I was working with a speaker's bureau that had another Jim Morris on its roster. He was a political comedian. We were both losing our minds until I finally decided to call the destination in Palm Springs where the speaking event was taking place.

"Do you want the baseball player or the comedian?" I asked.

"The comedian."

"Done."

I turned to the other Jim Morris and said, "You're up and I'm outta here. I'm going to church."

I chuckle when I think of what would have happened if we had both shown up at that event at the same time.

⁓

My speaking career began by accident. Speaking is something I've never been interested in nor would have ever pursued. But my agent Steve Canter was determined to turn me into a speaker prior to the release of *The Rookie*, to take advantage of the momentum once the film premiered. I resisted fiercely.

"I don't want to speak," I shot back. "I grew up not talking. I let my athletic performance do the talking. And now you're telling me I need to go out and make a living talking? Absolutely not, dude. Not doing that."

"You have a story to tell," Steve insisted. "Anyway, it's too late. I already booked you to speak before a group from Major League Soccer."

Actually, there were two speeches Steve locked me into. I won't reveal what I said in response; the language was far too blue. The first engagement was before 150 front office personnel from Major League Soccer—the body sanctioned by the United States Soccer Federation. That event was in

Dallas. The second one was before Del Monte Foods executives in Monterey, California.

"Talk for forty-five minutes," said Steve.

"I don't have anything to say," I deadpanned.

He suggested I write everything down beforehand. I didn't do that. I didn't want to speak.

I made the four-and-a-half-hour trip to Dallas for the Major League Soccer talk with Joel Engel, my coauthor for *The Oldest Rookie*. It was odd to say the least. After I was introduced, I mounted the stage in that hotel ballroom and just started spilling my guts, unleashing everything that happened to me. It was a stream of consciousness spiel. Those soccer people didn't move. They were engaged, enthralled really. I took that as a good sign and kept going. I unspooled for two-and-a-half hours, unlike anything I'm doing now.

When I finished, I was ecstatic. Joel was ecstatic. I had never talked that long before in my entire life. I signed autographs. I walked out and called Steve.

"What? You should never talk that long," he shouted. "Never more than an hour. You're going to write everything down you said and cut it down to an hour."

"Okay," I said.

I never wrote anything down.

These soccer people were offering me game tickets for whenever I had the opportunity to visit their cities. I didn't have the guts to tell them that I didn't even like soccer.

The reason I don't like the sport is far different from the reasons put forward by most people. It's not the pace of the game, or the lack of scoring, or the "Oh you just don't like soccer because you like football" canard. It's because of personal experience.

When I was a freshman in high school back in Hollywood, Florida, I loved playing soccer because it was a fast game. One of my good friends played with me as a goalie. During one contest, the opposing team kicked a solid shot toward our goal. As my friend went to block the shot, his heel slid over the top of the ball. The momentum forced his leg to the outside of the goal post just as another player was sliding into the ball. That player collided with the bottom part of his leg and wrapped it around the post.

The impact destroyed his knee. It tore everything there is to tear in that complex joint. "This is just not my game," I said to myself as my friend winced and screamed in pain. "Not my game."

I still didn't want to talk when I made the trip to Monterey. Why would these people, whose vegetables I had been eating since I was a baby, want me to talk to them? Nothing I had to say was worthy. I had a self-defeating attitude from the beginning, and I was still carrying a lot of painful baggage around from my childhood.

The Del Monte crowd numbered around 700. I took to heart the advice of my agent and kept the talk down to about an hour, though I discarded his suggestion to write everything down. I compressed the talk by glancing at my watch and calculating the number of stories I could tell within a one-hour timeframe.

Del Monte loved it. They paid me $25,000 to talk about how to overcome obstacles and how to surround yourself with good people. Because if you hang out with questionable people, I insisted, you're going to be viewed as questionable.

When the movie came out, the offers started pouring in. They came from big insurance and pharmaceutical companies, financial institutions, and telecommunications firms. We traveled anywhere and everywhere, from Bora Bora to Jamaica, Bermuda to Rome, and all the way to Switzerland. Back before the 2008 and 2009 financial collapse, I was speaking up to seventy times per year, and these organizations spent lavishly on the conferences where I spoke.

Then the meltdown hit. I had forty speeches scheduled. Twenty-nine of them got cancelled. All of those organizations that were hiring outside orators to headline their events decided to go with speakers from inside the company. It killed us. My speaking career slowed to a crawl. In 2007, we had moved from Fairview, Texas to Frisco into a 4,500-square foot house. It was decked-out—our dream house.

It featured a luxurious kitchen with commercial-style appliances, a large semi-circular office, a movie room with a projection screen, and hand-troweled, custom-painted walls. We had an adjustable rate mortgage with a $4,500 monthly payment for the first three months.

Then the year rolled over and the mortgage company discovered that they had screwed up: they forgot to include property taxes in the monthly payment. Our payment instantly jumped to $7,500 per month, just as my income stream was cratering.

Given the real estate market landscape at that time, there was no way we could sell the house to get out from under these crippling payments. We were face-to-face with bankruptcy and foreclosure. We were forced to turn in the keys. It was a gut-wrenching decision; it was the perfect house. But after everything got so upside down and sideways, I learned very quickly to dislike it. That house became a wart. Nobody likes warts.

So we packed up and moved to Kerrville, downsizing into a simple townhouse. At our bankruptcy hearing, very few of the lenders who expended us credit appeared in court to press their claims. The result was that almost half of our debt was canceled. We paid back the rest over the next two years. A dark chapter in our lives had closed.

∽

In 2001, Steve had suggested I hire this guy from Kansas City and fly him to Texas to teach me how to be a professional speaker. If I was going to pursue this as a career, I may as well learn the dos and don'ts from a pro—at least that was the thinking. I contacted him and signed a contract for a five-day intensive coaching session. I made arrangements for him to stay in a hotel right across the street from the Dallas apartment complex where I lived at the time. It featured an audio-visual room as a resident amenity.

After I picked the guy up at the airport and brought him to the complex, we took over the audio-visual room. He set up multiple cameras and recorders, sat in the back, and sent me to the front of the room.

"Okay. Start. Let's hear your story," he said.

After my talk, we sat down, reviewed the video, and he critiqued my performance. Then sent me to the front of the room to do it all over again.

"I can't teach you anything here," he said after my second go around. "The world does not need another Tony Robbins. The world needs good messages. You be *you*, and people will come to listen and learn. They're going to love you."

He gave me a few more pointers, a couple quick tips—never have facial hair—and went back to Kansas City after just a half a day. I still had to pay him his $5,000 fee though.

He was wrong about the facial hair, especially after the mop on the top of my head had mysteriously vanished. But he did give me the confidence I needed to grow into my new professional role. If God can use a stutterer (Moses) to address kings, and take a persecutor and turn him into an apostle (Saul of Tarsus, aka St. Paul), then who am I to doubt that God could take an introvert like me and have him speak for a living?

I wasn't quite sure where my ability came from. It seemed to come out of nowhere. I remembered my grandfather always said that you could learn more by listening than you could by talking. I took that to heart.

It wasn't until about five years ago that I learned from my Uncle Bob, my father's brother, that my grandfather had been a Toastmaster. And he could tell stories. I remember sitting around the table with my grandmother and grandfather, their best friends, and whoever else came over, just listening to everyone tell compelling stories.

What I remember most is that, when my grandfather spoke, everyone's eyes were glued to him. He had this charisma. It was like the old EF Hutton commercial: when Ernest talked, everyone listened. He was dry. He was hysterically funny. Sometimes, he would say something and people had to think for a second about what he had just said before it clicked. "Oh my God. You got me," they would say.

People would come into the store from in town and from out of state, and after the store was closed he would put the key in the front door and lock it. He would mix a drink for whoever stayed, and they would sit in the back of the store telling stories. I learned a lot during that period. That's where I got a lot of my speaking ability, soaking up those backroom stories.

When I'm speaking, I can usually tell if people are interested in what I'm saying or not. If not, I'll change things up to engage them. If I go in one direction and they bite into it, I'll stay on track. If I don't get the reaction I'm looking for, I'll change course—all on the fly.

When Disney sent me to Tokyo to debut *The Rookie*, I fell in love with the culture. It was the first place I had ever visited where if you tip people, they take it as an insult. They do their job because they're devoted to it. Japan allowed me to see how it should be done.

The Japanese absolutely love the game of baseball. I spoke in a big theater to a crowd of about 5,000 people before a screening of the movie. I had a Japanese interpreter on stage with me, and I would give my answer to each of her questions. She would then translate into Japanese, talking for about five minutes after each answer. The audience was laughing and giggling.

"What are you saying?" I asked.

"I'm taking care of you," she said.

A big part of me still wonders why people are so receptive to what I have to say. And it's something I'm determined to never take for granted. There are times when I have been sick and, before I go on stage, I have no voice at all. Yet when I get up there to speak, the words simply flow and I can even talk to people afterwards. But when I walk out of the facility, my voice has always disappeared again.

My grandfather always said if you are ever going to do anything, make sure you do it to the best of your ability. Because you don't want to wake up one day and ask, "What if I had tried just a little harder?"

So, even though I never write anything down before I speak, I'm able to pull relevant stories into my presentation that fit that situation, at that time and for that audience. It just kind of happens, all off the cuff.

And that's where my faith comes in. I just give it to God and say: "You just take over, man. You have me say whatever it is you want me to say, and reach whomever you want me to reach." It's been working this way for twenty years now.

Over the first three or four years I told my story, people were very receptive. That is until I went up to Saskatchewan, Canada to speak during a conference for the unemployed. Conferees were submitting resumes and filling out job applications. They had a full roster of speakers filling the whole day with speeches. By the time I was to appear, the conference was already two-and-a-half hours over schedule. These people were exhausted.

But as I was standing backstage waiting to go on, there was a lady speaking. She was lacing her talk with biting humor. The crowd roared with laughter. I myself was doubled over. That's when I realized that I needed humor to keep this thing going. I was in hockey country telling a dry baseball story for unemployed Canadians. What could go wrong?

I went on after her and it was miserable. I was making them think too hard. After my talk, they awarded me with a polite golf clap. It was a low point. But I learned from that experience.

Now I take my audiences up and down the scale, making them think really hard. At the same time, I make them laugh really hard too. We all do stupid stuff. And if I've done it, they've done it. Why not laugh about it? I want them to think, "Hey, I've been confronted with that. How did you handle it?" I've discovered that when people are laughing, they're really thinking.

I remember this speech I did for the Million Dollar Round Table in San Diego before 10,000 people. These were the top insurance company salespeople from around the world. This marked the first time I actually committed my speech to paper. I had to, because it had to strictly adhere to the twenty-five-minute time slot. Plus, they had to translate the speech into other languages because of all of the different people from different places in attendance.

They ate it up. There were people from Japan sitting in the front row right next to the stage. They were snapping my picture with their cameras and I thought, *this is what Godzilla must have felt like.*

· I just try to keep rolling with whatever is going on in the audience. Sometimes, when I'm speaking, a phone will go off and I'll say, "Hello?" Or, someone will sneeze and I'll say, "Bless you." I did this fundraiser for a private school in Austin, and as I got up to talk, a public address system speaker blew out making this horribly loud trumpet sound. I put my hand behind my bum and waved it back and forth. "Whoops, excuse me," I said, and kept going. The people were on the floor laughing.

I remember an engagement we had in Seoul, South Korea. I was giving a talk before a crowd where twenty-six different dialects were spoken. Everyone was wearing headphones so that they could hear my words translated into their particular dialect.

I discovered as I was speaking that each translation proceeded at a different pace. And so, when I told a joke, the laughter would go from one group to the next group and so on. It was like a domino effect. Different groups would be laughing at something I had said previously, even though I had moved on to a topic that was deadly serious. The laughs were wildly misplaced.

So I slowed down. I instinctively adjusted my cadence, pausing to make faces and gestures, acting out my words in an exaggerated fashion—like an actor. These movements made them laugh even more. And the translator looked at me and said, "How do you do that?"

I really don't know. It just happens. It's a gift. I've always been able to adapt on the fly. When I walk out, I know immediately when I've got people. When Shawna started travelling with me, she would sit in the audience and take note of how the audience reacted to my words. People would be talking, or looking at their phones, or clinking knives and forks against plates while eating, and shortly after I began my talk, the room would suddenly go dead silent. People were transfixed.

What I've always done is search the crowd for the one person in the room who seems bored and disinterested. I'd focus my attention on that one person. Once I get their attention and saw them laugh, I knew I had everybody in the room.

In my halcyon days before the 2008 crash, I spoke before a financial services company. The conference was in Tahiti—shabby, I know. We boarded a ship that had stops at the islands of French Polynesia. I was talking to this group one night during rough seas, and the forty-foot-tall curtains behind the stage were swaying one way, and I was going the other way, struggling to maintain my balance. All I could see when I looked out over the audience was the tops of people's heads. Not one person looked at me. Everyone bowed in seasickness. Fortunately, I've never suffered from motion-related afflictions.

For the next five days, the seas were calmer and we went on excursions to see volcanoes and the tropical landscape and went jet skiing, horseback riding, and four-wheeling. "I heard your speech," people would say to me. "Sounded awesome."

One of the strangest talks I ever gave—also one of my earliest speeches—was for Sprint Corporation. I gave a speech right on the beach in Kona, Hawaii. The attendees had been drinking for six hours. The sea was rough, and the waves were battering the beach so hard that it was difficult for the audience to hear me.

When I returned home, I found out that Sprint had just announced a massive layoff. I was pumping these people up on the beach in Hawaii, and they returned home and were handed pink slips. Maybe those people really did need to hear what I had to say through the crashing surf after all.

In 2018, I spoke before an audience of Pacific Gas & Electric employees, just before the Camp Wildfire that November—named after Camp Creek Road in Butte County, California. It was the most destructive and deadly wildfire in the state's history. It killed eighty-five people and destroyed much of the town of Paradise.

The fire was blamed on faulty PG&E transmission equipment, and potential liabilities from the fire drove the utility company into bankruptcy. Back during my speech, they were excited, engaged, and happy. Soon after, the same company is facing millions—maybe billions—of dollars in liability claims. Boy, do they need a motivational speech right now.

∞

When I give my talks, I believe I'm providing people with hope. My audiences see someone who has tried a lot, been through a lot, faltered a lot, and fought every step of the way. I've struggled my entire life—with an abusive father, an unsuccessful first marriage, attending college as an older person while supporting a family, and failing in the pursuit of my childhood dream before getting a chance to revisit that dream.

I receive almost universal praise for my talks. I'm often classified as the highest rated speaker ever for many of these organizations. What makes me so different from everyone else, I believe, is that I'm relatable. I'm the guy next door.

I'm not piously instructing the audience, saying "you need to do this" or "you need to do that." I make fun of all of the stupid choices I've made, and the foolish things I've done and how I've overcome them. I contrast these dumb moves with the things that I've done right and the success that has resulted. And I make people think.

It's cathartic, really. I talk about all of the crap that has happened to me, and people relate to it. I talk about my pain and sadness and what can go wrong when you quit living. If you fight obstacles and overcome them, good things will happen. If you can look back over your life and think, "What the hell was I doing? What was going through my mind?" you're in a pretty good spot.

This is my dream. This is my sports rush now—the more people, the better. Because if I can get them laughing, it's a much bigger noise.

My success at facing these challenges was not the result of anything I did. My triumphs were due to the fact that I was in a place God wanted me to be, and once I accepted that, things worked out.

When I first started speaking, people advised me that I should never talk about my faith. You can't discuss faith before corporate groups, they said. It will kill your public speaking career, I was told. These are businesspeople and they come from everywhere and have a variety of beliefs, they counseled.

One particular speaker's bureau informed me that if I insisted on speaking about my faith, they would not pay me and I would never get a speaking engagement through them again. Now, this same bureau sends me contracts with this anti-faith language marked out.

No one has ever responded negatively to anything faith-related I have ever said. People don't care. In fact, they crave this kind of message. Because if you don't have faith in something bigger than yourself, you're screwed.

I once spoke before a group of genetic scientists. I had to sign a contract that included a clause that said I couldn't talk about my faith. I did so anyway. The upshot? I missed a plane because 200 of these scientists—people who believe in nothing that can't be validated through mathematical equations and the scientific method—came to discuss faith with me after my talk. Something is going on there, and though I would love to say it's because I'm a great speaker, I know that's bull.

I don't want this to sound corny or highfalutin, but I believe that through my talks, I'm fighting for humanity. I want people to treat each other like they would treat their grandmother, like I was urged to treat my grandmother. I want humanity to know that they can be kind and that not everything is about you, the individual. Sometimes we need to contribute to something greater than ourselves. Giving of ourselves to others often helps us go further than we ever imagined we could. I want people to see that the human race is not in as bad a condition as we might think. Because a few bad people don't spoil the whole apple cart.

I think people realize that they can go far if they discard dream killers and surround themselves with dream makers. I want them to see what happens when you're not afraid to fail, when you're willing to get back up, dust yourself off, and chase your dream again. Because it's often not the dream you start out chasing that you end up loving the most. It's the one that reveals itself along the way.

People hear it; they love it, and they recommend me as a speaker to other groups. It's working one group at a time. My fifteen innings in the Major Leagues have been transformed into a twenty-year career of telling stories of hope and big dreams.

Whenever I commit to speaking before a group, I send the movie trailer and an introduction for the host organizations to use before I'm introduced. That introduction tells of my "meteoric rise" to the Major Leagues. On one occasion, the emcee misread the introductory script and told the audience of my "mediocre rise."

To some, the stories I'm currently living may seem mediocre. It's more compelling to talk about Major League success than it is to tell of the grind of living with physical ailments, pain, and opioid addiction. But God often uses mediocre stories for profound purposes. In fact, God seems to prefer the mediocre stories.

In scripture, Ruth was just a simple woman trying to provide food for herself and her mother-in-law when she gave birth to David's grandfather, a forbearer in the lineage of Jesus.

David was just a shepherd singing songs, tending sheep, and defending his flock. God anointed him king.

Mary was just an ordinary teenage girl before God— through the angel Gabriel—announced her divine selection as the mother of the Christ.

It's the mediocre stories of faith that draw us in. Whenever I sign autographs, I always include the verse from Hebrews 11:1: *Now faith is confidence in what we hope for and assurance about what we do not see.*

God isn't finished writing my story. I'm convinced He can use my narrative to give people the hope to live as their best selves. There may yet be another meteoric rise in this mediocre body. I don't know how my story ends, but I am confident that the ending God is writing is better than anything I can begin to imagine.

God has me on this path for a reason. My job is to follow that path until He reveals what I am to do next. I'm trying to do the best I can with what He has shown me He wants. And that's it.

CHAPTER 12

BE YOUR OWN DREAM MAKER

There are dream killers and dream makers. The world has far too many dream killers, and a dearth of dream makers. In my talks and through this book, I strive to elucidate the difference, and encourage people to aspire to dream maker status.

The path is difficult. When you step out to make a difference, you will face trials and the brutal force of resistance. Any effort to make changes in your life and in the lives of others will generate pushback. It's unavoidable. The only way we can free ourselves from this oppositional pushback is to sit back and do nothing. And this is not an option.

In the following pages I've listed seven principles of dream makers that I've teased out from my own triumphs and setbacks. There are no doubt more. But the important thing is to begin. The world needs you.

Harness the Power of Stories

We are a species driven by stories. Stories challenge the status quo and engage our imagination. Stories fuel personal growth and achievement. Stories teach us empathy and give us the courage to try new things and to do the impossible.

A good story will stick with you for years, much longer than any list of facts or a statistics-driven lecture. Stories reach deep into the human soul.

I tell my stories to encourage others to live out better lives. I take great pleasure in marshaling my words to bring out the best in others.

Stories take us along a journey buffeted by a range of emotions that can touch us deeply. When you immerse yourself in story, you forget yourself, suspend disbelief, and enter a feature film narrative, if you will. You transcend the narrow confines of your life. Stories make you think and see in new ways. If the storyteller can make the listener feel that the narrative they are hearing is a part of their own life because they've experienced similar things, they can laugh or cry about it and undergo a shift, sometimes a profound one. I've seen this happen time and time again.

We often lose sight of the enormous power of words. This power is why so many people today are passionately committed to suppressing—sometimes violently—the use of certain words.

God spoke all things into being. Jesus—the word made flesh—calmed the storms simply by saying so. The Bible is rife with examples of the life-giving power of words.

This is the power I tried to harness as a teacher and coach. Back when I was teaching, I encountered instances of other teachers speaking ill of some of the students. I'd remind them that they didn't know everything that student had to go through just to be in the classroom that day.

Maybe they were abused at home.

Maybe they were bullied in the bathroom.

Maybe they didn't get dinner last night, or breakfast that morning.

Maybe they were ridiculed on their way out the door.

I've lived some of those same struggles and I know this same exact pain. I choose to believe the best in people because I think people often live up or down to expectations. I want people to be their best. And people are desperate for inspiring stories of hope.

Seek out stories that uplift you personally. More importantly, discover what words hold power and meaning for you and strive to be the author of your own inspiring narrative. Write it down in ink on paper. The fate of humanity may depend on it.

Don't Waste Your Time on Perfect

Over the years, I've learned that there is only one perfect person who has ever walked the face of the earth. And it's not me. We're wasting our time if we pursue perfection, because no one can be perfect. It's a recipe for pain.

If you're looking for perfect, you're a hostage to single-mindedness. You're blinded to whatever else is going on around you and the people moving in and out of your life. You'll miss crucial opportunities and what it is you were meant to do and be. The dream you start chasing with your quest for perfection might not be the one you end up loving the most. It's not the destination, but the journey that fulfills us and makes us who we are.

The pursuit of perfection blinds us to the truth that our dreams transform over time. After I had a family, actualizing my dream of playing professional baseball receded and was never as important to me as my kids were. My ambitions shifted from having what I wanted when I wanted it, to a passionate desire to give my kids what they needed when they needed it. Having kids was a dream I didn't even know I wanted until it fell into my lap—unintentionally.

I've always loved the freedom and self-discovery that can be found in competitive sports. Sports teach us that there is no such thing as perfect. On the field or off, the hunt for perfection is a cruel fallacy, one that casts us into despair when we fall short—as we most assuredly will.

The best we can hope for is feeling a sense of satisfaction that comes from successfully competing against ourselves, making ourselves better through effort and passion, and being a good teammate. Accept your shortcomings and learn to live in—and enjoy—the moment. We put so much pressure on ourselves and on our kids in a futile quest to be perfect that we have forgotten how to experience the gift of now. Sports help us lean into and fully live out each and every moment.

As a speaker, I'm not trying to be motivational power-house Tony Robbins or Christian orator Max Lucado. I'm trying to be the best Jim Morris I can possibly be. That's all God wants for us. He wants us to be the unique creations we were born to be, accepting of our imperfections as we strive to live out his will. This is the message that truly resonates with people.

Give of Your Gifts

One of my grandfather's most oft repeated adages was "live for other people." That is the true definition of a dream maker. *What* you support pales in comparison to *whom* you are supporting. If you can remember who you are and whose you are, your support for others rings true. You're doing it right. You can change lives.

I remember on the third day of baseball practice after I started coaching in Big Lake, one of the dads approached me. "My kid did not sign up for baseball to pick weeds on the field," he said. So, on the fourth day of practice, that dad was picking weeds. Followed by more dads. Followed by teachers.

You respect things a whole lot more if you earn them by diligently tending to the details, no matter how menial they might be. That baseball field was our home. Teams were coming to beat us in our home. We weren't going to have that. Those kids respected that field because they gave their effort, doing the work to maintain it themselves. We won every home game that championship season.

How many of those kids from that winning season played baseball after graduating from Reagan County High School? None. But most of them learned how to dream. Some of those kids call me on occasion. They're part of a nonprofit I created. Our first year, we supported the athletic program at O. D. Wyatt High School in Fort Worth. The objective is to get kids onto the ball field and teach life lessons through the game of baseball.

"Coach, we're as old now as you were when you tried out," they said.

"Shut up," I said.

My third baseman flies helicopters for the Coast Guard just outside of Houston. When talking to him one night, I told him I'd like him to take me for a ride in his helicopter.

"Sure coach," he quipped. "Just take a boat out into the bay, turn it over, and I'll come get you."

Up to the age of thirty-five, I failed every single attempt I made to reach my dream. But when I pressed that group of kids to be the best they could be, they showed me how to dream again. When I pushed them, they pushed back. And we *all* became better for it.

It doesn't matter how old or how young you are. When you help somebody else, it changes your life. You get a feeling like no other.

The more we share—whether it's money, time, or talent—the more abundance we experience in life. The more we give, the more we are healed. Give your gifts. And don't take anything for granted. Be eternally grateful for what you have. The opportunities for giving and expressing gratitude are endless.

In August of 2015, I received a compelling vision while praying in church. In it, I was riding a bicycle across the United States. In each city along the way, I'd connect with communities and organize youth sports camps for kids in need. I'd invite celebrities and musical guests to highlight the project. My goal was to provide an alternative to gangs and poverty—to encourage these kids and others to overcome the obstacles they faced as they chased their biggest dreams.

To turn this vision into reality, I formed the Jim "The Rookie" Morris Foundation that same month. I bought a stationary bike to get into shape. We talked about the project wherever we went, and people started handing us business cards, offering their support and resources.

We named the bike ride the "Ride 2 Restoration." It hasn't happened yet, but the hope is that by riding bikes a few thousand miles and seeding youth sports camps, we'll gain national attention. The president and CEO of Baptist Children Family Services (BCFS) met with us and offered us their services, including one of their buses, first aid ambulances, their logistics team, and semis, tents, and booths. Chris Avery of James Avery Artisan Jewelry offered us support. Even the MLB Players Alumni Association wanted to help.

That first year of the foundation, we funneled practically everything we earned into the project. Through my friend Terry Drake, we connected with the athletic director and head football coach and the baseball coach at O. D. Wyatt High School in Fort Worth. We toured the school and saw a facility in dire need. The weight room was just an old locker room. Free weights were stacked on a cement floor. Their only medicine ball was torn. How were athletes supposed to train in these conditions? Who would put in the sweat and hard work with equipment that might cause injury?

Everything was old and needed to be refurbished or replaced, from the uniforms to the ball field. While developing a strategy to support the high school, my foundation held its first event: "Between the White Lines" sports camp. The Texas Rangers sent out players to help with baseball drills. It was incredible. There were several components to the program. We worked through baseball and football drills and best practices for the sport. We also fed the athletes two meals and gave them motivational support.

Thanks to Chris Avery and James Avery Artisan Jewelry, we were able to help rebuild a run-down field and acquire new sporting equipment. We purchased weight machines and flooring for their weight room. Through donations of time and sports equipment from Thrivent Financial and Play it Forward, the school's athletic program got a much-needed boost. A little more than a year after I received that vision, we had reworked the netting for the batting cages, acquired tools for continuing field maintenance, and allocated two full sets of new uniforms for the baseball team along with bats, balls, and pitching machines. We also provided the softball team with new equipment.

In October of 2016, we held a public event to unveil our work: "Meet Me on the Mound." NASCAR driver Michael McDowell, who at the time drove the Leavine Family Racing #95 Chevrolet, along with the racing team from Thrivent Financial—McDowell's sponsor—joined me at O. D. Wyatt for a softball game. We followed the game with a question and answer session from the crowd. Admission was free, but attendees were encouraged to donate new or gently used sporting equipment.

As athletes, Michael and I are both competitive to the core. My team came out ahead in the end, but I might have had a slight advantage as we were competing on my turf instead of his.

Laugh at Yourself

One day, not long after my grandfather was diagnosed with ALS, I was stacking shirts on the shelves in his clothing store. And when I say "stack," I mean I was perched on a ladder with a ruler in my hand, arranging them precisely the way my grandfather wanted. I was making sure each shirt stack was consistent and precisely spaced.

As I was stretching with the ruler to check my work, a lady walked into the store. I turned around to get a glimpse of her and when I did, I lost my balance on the ladder and came crashing down onto three shelves of meticulously stacked shirts. I expected my grandfather to be furious with me because, for the first fifteen years of my life, each of my mistakes was met with rage.

I got up. My cheeks were red with embarrassment. I turned around to look at my grandfather, and when I did, he was laughing so hard he almost fell out of his wheelchair.

"Come here," he said motioning me to approach.

"Look, life is hard," he said. "And if you're making mistakes, that means you're trying to accomplish something. If you're not goofing up, you've given up. Making a mistake puts you one step closer to where you want to be. Don't take things so seriously. Have fun with what you're doing. Things are going to happen in your life and people are going to laugh at you."

"What do I do?" I asked.

"You laugh back," he said.

"Why would I laugh at myself?"

"Because then people will think you're crazy, and they will leave you alone."

But that wasn't my most monumental gaffe. *That* happened on April 12, 2000 at Tropicana Field in St. Petersburg, Florida. I was pitching against the Chicago White Sox. The contest was broadcast on ESPN and was the network's

Game of the Week. There were 40,000 people in the stands and millions more watching the game on television.

It was the top of the sixth inning, and I was facing slugger and designated hitter Frank Thomas, "The Big Hurt," at a time when Thomas could really hit. I had just struck out shortstop Jose Valentin. Caught him looking. The count was 2 and 2, and our catcher, Johnny Flaherty, called for a slider.

I set, and as I lifted my right leg to begin the windup, the spike of my right shoe got caught in the lace of my left shoe. I lost my balance and fell down in slow motion. I threw the ball exactly twelve inches. Every dirty word I could think of flashed in front of me. I thought to myself, *Dude, you did not just fall down on national TV.*

I didn't want to look toward the plate. I knew they were laughing. I knew the people in the stands were laughing. So, I nonchalantly dusted myself off and spit the dirt out of my mouth. "Not that bad," I said to myself. Then I started laughing. I busted out so hard I cried.

As I got my composure back, I straightened my hat, and stood back up on the mound. Standing on top of home plate was Thomas, laughing hysterically. Behind him was my catcher Flaherty. He had his back to me. All I could see were his shoulders bouncing up and down as his body shook. The umpire had his mask off and was wiping tears from his eyes.

After he recovered, Thomas stepped back into the batter's box. Flaherty gave me a sign, I set, lifted my leg—I did not trip—and released. He took it for strike three. I caught him looking. As Thomas walked back to the dugout he stopped halfway, looked toward me, and tipped his cap. Then he winked at me, and started giggling.

I threw two innings that night in a game we lost 7 to 1. When I went into the clubhouse after the game to toss my glove into my locker, there was a sign: "Did you have a nice fall?" Underneath that was a post-it note stuck to a VHS videotape: "Just a little gift from the guys at ESPN," It said. That videotape contained a recording of me falling down every which way on the mound: forwards, backwards, and in fast and slow motion.

It was played for the next six days of our home stand on the centerfield screen during batting practice. That's an hour-and-a-half every day.

After I showered and got dressed, I walked out of the locker room. Frank Thomas was outside the door waiting for me. He threw his arm around me. "I'm taking you out to eat," he said, giggling.

"I don't know why you're laughing. You struck out," I said.

"I strike out all the time. You fell down on national TV."

Don't take life so seriously that you forget to have fun. Don't get so caught up moving between point A and point B that you miss a door that might take you to another dream. We're going to screw up. Sometimes you've just got to laugh. And get on with the journey.

Don't Lose Your Humble

When I went into The Treatment Center of the West Palm Beaches, my patient advocate Sonja kept advising me:

"Don't lose your humble." I was judging the people who came into the center, those who looked like death warmed over. "That was you just a few weeks ago," she would admonish.

For every single person on this planet, and especially for those of us who are addicts, change is incredibly hard. Every step on our journey through life requires a willingness to change. Those who were at the center for the third, fourth, or fifth time didn't learn how to change. Something difficult would happen in their lives, something that would make them feel bad, and they sought comfort and escape from life's challenges by returning to their addictions. They didn't change. They gave up on themselves.

I myself coasted through life for a long time. I rested on my past successes instead of looking ahead to new adventures and new dreams. I forgot that God put me here on this planet to give of my talents for others. When you coast, you quit growing. You get comfortable—too comfortable—and this makes change difficult. You resist change, even if God is the one leading the changes.

Every single day at the center I was surrounded by all of these amazing, beautiful people who gave up on themselves. I was tempted to point fingers and judge. I wanted to curse Big Pharma. I wanted to call out the mistakes and laziness of doctors. I wanted to vilify everything that put these people in this predicament. Then I looked in the mirror and remembered who and where I was.

Don't lose your humble, Morris.

I thought I might get Sonya's new motto for me printed on a T-shirt. I don't know what the design would look like.

Maybe a stick figure wearing a tight shirt and white tube socks pulled up to the knees, with arrows pointing to all of my surgeries and labels denoting all of the drugs I was addicted to. Or maybe it's a picture of me on a pitcher's mound watching a home run disappear into the night sky. Or maybe it should be a silk-screened image of me performing naked jumping jacks.

I've tried to take control of my life, trusting in my own pride and power, and it nearly destroyed me. To be humble is not to discount any of the things you've done. To be humble is to remember the one who created us and calls on us to follow his example.

> *All of you, clothe yourselves with humility toward one another because, "God opposes the proud, but gives grace to the humble." Humble yourselves, therefore, under God's mighty hand, that he may lift you up in due time.*

—1 Peter 5:5–6.

Before I step out onto the stage now, I ask God to speak to the hearts of those gathered to hear my story. "God, speak through me."

I tell my story to help people remember their dreams, to help them figure out who they are. When we forget who we are and what makes our hearts redound with passion, when we lose sight of those things that give us love and hope for better tomorrows, we lose our way and fall into despair.

Don't lose your humble.

Life is tough. The older you get, the harder it becomes. Brains and bodies slow down, not moving as quickly or as adeptly as before. Everyone has been through good times. Each of us has suffered pain. Every life is full of mountaintop highs, and Death Valley desert lows. The goal of life is not to reach a mountaintop high and try to stay there, to vainly try and keep everything perfect. It's to keep living when the obstacles come crashing in, to muster the determination to find a way to overcome those setbacks, and to share your successes with others and learn from your failures. That's what makes a good life story.

This is one of the great lessons of baseball. Do you have the courage to stay in the game, to dust yourself off and get back on the field when the play is hard, and the game humiliates you?

When I've screwed up, when I've chased ghosts down rabbit trails, when I've ignored God in my life, God is still able to keep working through the circumstances and redeem my blunders for a better story.

There is a misconception that the life of a traveling motivational speaker is full of comfort and ease. Nothing could be further from the truth. I've driven through hurricanes to try and get to my engagements. I've been behind the wheel for twenty-four hours straight in an effort to honor my commitments. I've slept in airports and tried not to think about what may or may not be on the carpet. I've slept in spartan cabins and in luxurious coastal suites, and in vehicles of every make, model, and color.

From gate-to-gate and state-to-state, not losing my humble has been a great and wise motto for finding my way.

He guides the humble in what is right and teaches them his way. —Psalm 25:9.

Don't lose your humble.

One of the most profound "don't lose your humble" lessons I've learned is that it isn't about *me*. It's about *we*. When you look at each situation not as an opportunity to benefit yourself but as a possibility to contribute to others and to something greater, things change profoundly.

An agreement or a business arrangement isn't about what you can get out of it; it's about benefitting everyone involved. A marriage isn't about the personal satisfaction the union brings to you; it's about what you bring to the marriage and how you contribute to its lasting success. Individuals who enter into matrimony with visions of what the marriage will do for them are doomed to bitter disappointment.

When you work as *we*, everyone involved is better, and a lot stronger. Gordon Wood, the legendary coach of the Brownwood Lions football team, taught me that it doesn't matter how big, strong, and fast you are. He always stressed that if you have more heart, have a better plan, and work as a team, you're going to win.

And win we did. The night we won the 1981 Texas High School Football Championship, the team we competed against had a guy who was averaging 275 yards running the ball in the first half of each game that year. That team was the Fort Bend Eagles, now the Sugar Land Willowridge Eagles. That player was Thurman Thomas.

We held the future NFL running back and Pro Football Hall of Famer in check the entire game. We knew what he was going to do before he did, because we were prepared, we had the plan, we had the heart, and we worked as a team.

They were bigger, they were faster, and they were stronger. But we found a way to win, and we did so by a score of 14 to 9. The next year, Thomas led his team to win the AAAA state championship.

God is writing a great story for each of us. Learn to be the best you can be in this great story. And *don't lose your humble.*

Listen for God

Over the July Fourth weekend of 1994, my nationally-ranked softball team made the trip to Albuquerque, New Mexico for a critical regional tournament. My mother-in-law stayed with our kids, allowing my wife Lorri to accompany me. These tournaments were really the only time we spent together without the kids.

I was in the shower after a tournament game when one of my teammates delivered some terrible news. My best friends John Mark Davidson, a tight end on the Angelo State University football team, and Rob McClellan, a resident assistant in the dorm where I worked as director, had been in an accident. They were on their way to another softball tournament in a recreational league in Sanderson, Texas, when John Mark's new Jeep Wrangler overturned. That Jeep had an open top. Rob was killed. John Mark was in critical condition. No other cars were involved.

I quickly dressed and we drove all night back to San Angelo. When I walked into John Mark's hospital room, his father hugged me.

"We waited for you," he said. John Mark was on life support. There was no chance for recovery. They had been keeping him alive for two days awaiting my arrival so I could say my goodbyes.

His face was bruised and bandaged, and there were tubes sticking out of him. His chest rose and fell in sync with the respirator. How exactly do you say goodbye to your best friend like that? His father nodded to the doctor and, moments later, John Mark's heart registered a flat line on the monitor. He was twenty-five. I would have been with them in that Jeep had I not committed to playing in the tournament in Albuquerque.

Not long after his death, I came across a picture of John Mark standing next to a school bus. He drove that bus to pick up extra cash while attending Angelo State. The number of that bus was clearly visible in the photograph. That number was sixty-three.

I didn't know it then, but that number would assume profound significance in my life. When I got called up to the big leagues, the Devil Rays assigned me the number sixty-three. I didn't give it much thought at the time; there was no rhyme or reason to it. It was just a coincidence.

But then something startling happened while I was writing *The Oldest Rookie* with coauthor Joel Engel.

"How many kids came out for the baseball team the year you won the district championship?" Joel asked.

"I don't know," I responded. "Let me look it up." It turned out, sixty-three kids came out for that team. When was the last time Reagan County High School won a baseball championship before that? To my knowledge, they had never won a championship.

"Hey, that's no coincidence," Joel said.

In the years after *The Rookie*, while traveling to speaking engagements all over the country and the world, that number kept popping up. During a particularly rough stretch, I was driving down the highway by myself. It was early morning and I had a few hundred miles to cover if I was to get to my speaking event on time. I was completely exhausted. I was lost in my thoughts, praying as I drove, carrying on a conversation with God.

Is this what I'm supposed to be doing? What else can I do?

I wasn't completely focused on my driving, and I soon found myself stuck behind a slow-moving semi. I grew frustrated at first. Then I saw a sign posted on the back of the trailer.

"Our most precious cargo sits sixty-three feet ahead," it said.

The number could not have been printed any bigger. As odd as it sounds, that sign felt like a message straight from God: "You are my precious cargo, and you are on the right path. Just keep going."

A short time later, I was on a Southwest Airlines flight, just before takeoff, on my way to an event in Corpus Christi. I was tired. I didn't want to talk to anyone. I didn't want to speak at the event. So I prayed.

God, if you really want me to keep doing this you've got to tell me, because I'm tired and I don't want to do it. I don't know why you have me talking to people.

Just then, the flight attendant from the front of the plane walked to the back to meet the other flight attendant who was standing next to my row.

"Is everyone on board?" she asked.

"Yes, all sixty-three passengers are on board," the other flight attendant answered.

One of my first speaking engagements was at Preston Road Church of Christ in Dallas. It was right after *The Rookie* was released. I spoke on a Sunday.

The following Tuesday, I received a letter from the church. It said that in the church's sixty-three-year history, no speaker had ever filled the church like I did.

Then there was the time in the Black Hills of South Dakota. The event was at mile marker sixty-three, it was sixty-three degrees outside, and I ended up speaking before sixty-three people. Does that number hold special meaning? What is God trying to convey? Sometimes we miss what is right in front of us.

There's that old joke about a very religious man who was caught in rising floodwaters. He climbed onto the roof of his house and put his trust in God to rescue him. A neighbor came by in a canoe.

"The waters will soon be above your house. Hop in and we'll paddle to safety," the neighbor said.

"No thanks," replied the religious man. "I've prayed to God and I'm sure he will save me."

A short time later, the police came by in a boat. "The waters will soon be above your house," an officer said. "Hop in and we'll take you to safety."

"No thanks," replied the religious man. "I've prayed to God and I'm sure he will save me."

Not long after that, a rescue services helicopter hovered overhead and let down a rope ladder.

"The waters will soon be above your house," a crew-member shouted. "Climb the ladder and we'll fly you to safety."

"No thanks," the religious man shouted back. "I've prayed to God and I'm sure he will save me."

The floodwaters continued to rise, until soon they were above the roof. The man drowned. When he arrived in heaven the man demanded an audience with God. "Lord, why am I here in heaven?" the man asked. "I prayed for you to save me, I trusted you to save me from that flood."

"Yes you did, my child," replied the Lord. "And I sent you a canoe, a boat, and a helicopter. But you never got in."

God talks to us frequently and in many ways. He speaks through songs, people, numbers, and symbols—even movies. For every person, his mode of communication is different. We just have to be aware of his presence and be willing to listen.

What does sixty-three mean? I'm not a numerologist, but I believe God has used that number to continuously remind me of His presence. It's also been said that the angel number sixty-three indicates that you are on the correct life path for the fulfillment of your highest potential. That makes sense.

If God can use burning bushes (through which He spoke to Moses on Mount Horeb), talking donkeys (Balaam's ass, Numbers 22:28), and stars in the sky (the star of Bethlehem) to convey his messages, I'm convinced He can also use a few well-placed sixty-threes to nudge me along the way.

Remember Who You Are

Back during a time when men wore three-piece suits to work, my grandfather would call out to me every day—for three years—as I walked out the front door headed to school.

"Jimmy, remember who you are," he would say while buttoning his vest.

As an arrogant, know-it-all teenager, that saying bothered me. I heard those words and interpreted them as, "If you embarrass me in any way, I will kill you." My dad's violent anger greatly influenced how I received my grandfather's words.

It wasn't until I watched the group of high school kids I coached celebrate a district baseball championship they did not think they could win that I finally understood what my grandfather meant.

"Remember who you are."

It wasn't an attack or a threat. Those words were meant to challenge and encourage me to live a life full of character and integrity. When I walked out that front door, when I was walking the halls of the school, or the ball field, or wherever I might be, the actions I undertook when no one else was watching, that's when I needed to remember who I was. My grandfather, who possessed more personal character than any single person I have ever known, was trying to teach me how to cultivate honor and virtue.

For fifteen years, I'd borne witness to my parent's destructive marriage. They regularly hurled blows, curses, objects, and unbelievably ugly insults at each other.

For the next three years, while living under my grandparents' roof, I saw what living out faith on a daily basis looks like. Sure, they had fights, but they never said a cross word to each other. They were from the greatest generation. They worked hard and respected each other deeply. They knew the power of words. Hence, they never purposefully said anything to each other they would later want to take back.

That concept was so foreign to me.

I grew up with someone who was always casting blame on others, who never accepted responsibility for his actions, and whose failures were always someone else's fault. Some days it was like watching a two-year-old in a grown man's body throw a temper tantrum.

The first two lessons my grandfather taught me were simple: if you do it, you own it; and if you always tell the truth, you won't have to remember what you said.

Today's politicians and newsmakers could learn a few things from his maxims. Tell the truth. Mean what you say. Live and work with honor and respect. Do things the right way. Treat others the way you want them to treat you. Do it and own it.

Always remember that you stand for a whole lot more than just yourself. You stand for your family, your community, your state, and your God. Whatever it is you're representing, you are a part of it. Remember who you are at all times, because there are always others watching. It's not what you do when other people are watching that makes you who you are; it's what you do when no one can observe your actions.

Through my rollercoaster of a life, I remembered along the way who I was, who God made me to be. I recommitted myself to live out my grandfather's words, to live out his legacy for the rest of my life.

Remember who *you* are.

ACKNOWLEDGMENTS

To the Walt Disney Company, thank you for your belief and beautiful retelling of my story in *The Rookie*.

Dennis Quaid, thank you for your expertise and craftsmanship in portraying me so well. Most of all, thank you for your friendship over the years.

Joel Engel, I appreciate your hard work in digging out the memories and putting my story on paper for the first time.

Thank you to our God Talk Prayer "girls" for praying for Shawna and me at the drop of a hat—all hours of the day and night. I am convinced your prayers were and are a pivotal part of my healing.

Nena Madonia Oshman, your tenacity has challenged me and inspired me to write what was on my heart. Thank you for that push. And, Savio Republic folks, thank you for not giving up on me. It's taken years to get to this point.

Mark Stuertz, you are a master of words. Thank you for your partnership in this book. I look forward to future projects.

Kari Short, thank you for the countless hours of questions and answers and for your gift of putting words together. You believed in the importance of this story; I am grateful.

Thank you, Ethan Bryan, for your help in putting one of my most difficult seasons into words. You are an excellent storyteller.

Last but not least, to our adult children—Zach and Chelsea, Hunter and Lauren and baby Lily, Jessica, Chelsey, Jaimee, and John. Thank you for loving us, for running to our aid when we needed it most, for checking on us, and for praying. We love you all so very much.

Photo by Jodi Carpenter

ABOUT THE AUTHOR

Jim "The Rookie" Morris is a testament to the power of dreams and the capacity of aspirational visions to inspire and transform. His personal saga chronicles a meteoric rise from thirty-five-year-old high school teacher and coach in Big Lake, Texas, to flame-throwing relief pitcher for the Tampa Bay Devil Rays. His unlikely and brief Major League career took him from the Rays in 1999 and 2000 to the Los Angeles Dodgers in 2001, before a throwing arm injury forced him to retire.

His book *The Oldest Rookie* traces this improbable back-road trajectory to the Big Leagues. *The Rookie*, the feature film based on Morris' book and starring Dennis Quaid, was a critically acclaimed box office smash when the Walt Disney Company released it in 2002.

Today, Morris travels the world as one of America's foremost inspirational and motivational speakers. His appearances include prestigious events such as The Million Dollar Round Table and numerous professional speaker showcases.

Overcoming crippling barriers such as an unstable upbringing, an abusive father, severe injuries, and addiction, his incredible journey to the pitcher's mound and back is an affirmation of the inexplicable power of faith. His story has empowered hundreds of thousands of people to successfully tackle life's most vexing challenges and live out their dreams.

His story serves as a robust platform for philanthropic efforts that have included partnerships with Arms of Hope; BCFS, Community Services Division, Health & Human Services; Boys & Girls Clubs of America; Boy Scouts of America; Play It Forward USA, Keller Founding chapter; and the Texas Youth Commission. In September 2015, he launched the Jim "The Rookie" Morris Foundation (www. JTRMFoundation.org) to serve impoverished communities across America.

A father to five children and grandfather to one grandchild, Morris lives with his wife Shawna in San Antonio, Texas.

ABOUT THE CO-AUTHOR

A nationally award-winning journalist, Mark Stuertz has been a Dallas-based writer and author for more than twenty-five years. His writing has appeared in a variety of publications including the *Dallas Observer, Texas Monthly, American Way, Spirit, Food & Wine,* and *American Driver.* He is the author of *Secret Dallas: A Guide to the Weird, Wonderful, and Obscure,* and editor of the *Fearless Critic Dallas Restaurant Guide.*